TOTALLY TUBEYS!

24 Storytimes with Tube Crafts

Priscella Morrow

UpstartBooks

Fort Atkinson, Wisconsin

*This book is dedicated to all of you I have met, or have yet to meet,
who believe that learning can be fun!*

Credits:

The following organization has generously given permission to reprint songs and fingerplays in this book:

Pages 34, 48, 50, 53 and 78: Original authors unknown. Reprinted with permission of Preschool Education. *www.preschooleducation.com*

Published by UpstartBooks
W5527 Highway 106
P.O. Box 800
Fort Atkinson, Wisconsin 53538-0800
1-800-448-4887

© Priscella Morrow, 2003
Cover design: Jill Schroeder

The paper used in this publication meets the minimum requirements of American National Standard for Information Science — Permanence of Paper for Printed Library Material. ANSI/NISO Z39.48-1992.

Contents

Introduction

At last—fun new projects to enhance your storytime and craft programs! This book contains a collection of 24 storytimes and 27 Tubey crafts designed to give you creative ideas for special celebrations throughout the year. Each storytime includes an annotated bibliography, activity ideas, a Tubey pattern and instructions for each Tubey.

The storytime programs have been compiled for educators working with children from preschool through third grade, but the Tubeys can be enjoyed by children of all ages.

About Tubeys

Tubeys are easy to make. They are made from readily available and inexpensive materials. The base of each Tubey is the cardboard tube from a roll of bathroom tissue. The other materials needed are: construction paper scraps in various colors, scissors, black felt marker, single hole punch and glue. Optional tools are: star punch, heart punch, scallop-edge scissors and your imagination. The specified colors may be changed and adapted for your particular use and colored paper supply.

Tubeys can be used as a remembrance of your presentation, puppets to re-enact a story, display items, decorations, favors, hanging mobiles, etc. Children might also like to make a Tubey of themselves to use for a desk marker at Open House. The ways Tubeys can be used are limited only by your imagination.

Let's get started!

Tubey Pattern Basics

Before You Start

Make a photocopy of each pattern page. Roughly cut out each piece, leaving about one inch around the edges. Staple each piece inside the lines to an old manila folder. Then cut out each piece along the outline. This is your pattern. Place each pattern on the designated color of construction paper, trace around it and cut the piece out. Once you have cut out all of the pieces, you're ready to start your Tubey.

Basic Tube

Use a cardboard tube from a roll of bathroom tissue or cut 4½ inch tubes from paper towel or wrapping paper tubes.

Basic Small Tube

Cut a cardboard tube from a roll of bathroom tissue in half so it measures 2¼ inches or cut a 2¼ inch tube from a paper towel or wrapping paper tube.

Basic Hat

1. Cut slits along the bottom edge of Piece 2 as indicated on the pattern.

2. Overlap the short ends of Piece 2 and glue them together.

3. Fold the slit pieces into the hat. Apply glue to the folded edges, then press them onto Piece 1.

4. Use the eraser end of a pencil to tap the folded edges down until the glue dries.

Basic Patterns

Basic Tube Cover

Basic Small Tube Cover

Basic Patterns (continued)

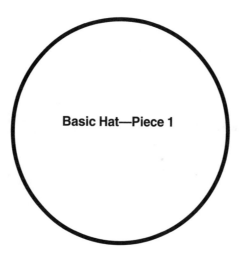

Basic Hat—Piece 1

Basic Hat—Piece 2

Cut Lines

Snowmen

Children love making snowmen. This storytime helps you bring the fun of snowmen inside, with stories, fingerplays, snowmen tubeys and more.

Books to Enjoy

Snowmen at Night by Caralyn Buehner. Putnam, 2002. (PK–1) A delightful story about the nocturnal activities of snowmen.

Our Snowman by M. B. Goffstein. Harper & Row, 1986. (PK–1) The snowman the children build looks so lonely that a little girl and her father go out and make him a wife.

The Snowy Day by Ezra Jack Keats. Viking Press, 1996. (PK–1) The adventures of a little boy in the city on a very snowy day.

First Snowfall by Anne and Harlow Rockwell. Aladdin Books, 1992. (PK–1) A child enjoys the sights and activities of a snow-covered world.

Henry and Mudge and the Snowman Plan by Cynthia Rylant. (K–3) Simon & Schuster, 1999. Henry, his dog Mudge and his father enter a snowman-building contest at the local park and win third place.

Snow Pumpkin by Carole Schaefer. Crown, 2000. (PK–1) When it snows in October, two friends build a snowman using a pumpkin as its head.

All You Need for a Snowman by Alice Schertle. Harcourt, 2002. (PK–K) Lists everything one needs to build the perfect snowman.

Fingerplay

Five Fat Snowmen

Five fat snowmen standing by my door,
(Hold up five fingers.)
One snowman melted and then there were four.
(Hold up four fingers.)
Four fat snowmen standing by the tree,
One snowman melted and then there were three.
(Hold up three fingers.)
Three fat snowmen looking at you,
One snowman melted and then there were two.
(Hold up two fingers.)
Two fat snowmen standing in the sun,
One snowman melted and then there was one.
(Hold up one finger.)
One SMALL snowman standing in the sun,
One snowman melted,
(Slowly sink to the floor.)
And then there were none!

Act it Out

Pretend to roll snowballs. First roll a big one, then a medium one, then a small one. Set them on top of each other to make a snowman. Ask, "What can we use for the eyes?... for the nose?... for the mouth?..." "What else does he need to keep him warm?" After the snowman is finished, he starts to melt. Ask, "What will be left when the snowman melts?"

Snowman Tubey

Parts You'll Need

- Basic Tube Cover (White)
- Basic Hat Pieces 1 and 2 (Black)
- Snowman Scarf (Green or Red)
- Snowman Nose (Orange)
- 2 Holly Leaves (Green)
- 2 Snowman Arms (Brown)

Materials You'll Need

- cardboard tube, 4½ inches tall
- construction paper
- scissors
- glue
- black marker
- single hole punch

Directions

1. Cover the tube with the white tube cover. Overlap the ends and glue them together.

2. Make the hat following the instructions on page 6.

3. Hole punch three red dots for holly berries and five black dots for the eyes, mouth and buttons.

4. Glue the holly leaves and berries to the hat.

5. Glue the eyes, nose and mouth to the front of the snowman.

6. Glue the scarf just below the snowman's mouth. The fringe should be in the front.

7. Glue the buttons below the scarf.

8. Fold the arms along the fold line. Glue each folded end to one of the snowman's sides. The arms should stick out on the sides.

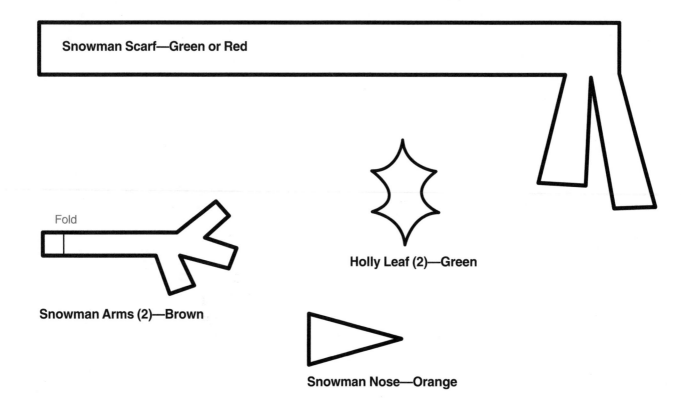

Snowman Scarf—Green or Red

Fold

Snowman Arms (2)—Brown

Holly Leaf (2)—Green

Snowman Nose—Orange

Penguins

Penguins are fun animals for children to learn about. The Animal Information Database on the SeaWorld Web site (www.seaworld.org/infobooks/Penguins/home.html) offers information about penguins that you can use to enhance your storytime.

Books to Enjoy

Cuddly Dudley by Jez Alborough. Candlewick Press, 1993. (PK–1) Tired of being surrounded by a family who always wants to cuddle him, Dudley the penguin leaves home so he can be alone.

The Penguin that Hated the Cold adapted by Barbara Brenner. Random House, 1973. (PK–K) Pablo the Penguin hates the cold so he decides to move to a tropical climate.

If I Were a Penguin by Heidi Goennel. Little, Brown, 1989. (PK–1) A child imagines the fun of being different animals.

Tackylocks and the Three Bears by Helen Lester. Houghton Mifflin, 2002. (K–3) Tacky the penguin and his friends perform a play for the little penguins in Mrs. Beakly's class, but with Tacky in the lead role, things do not go exactly as planned. Part of the Tacky the Penguin series.

Penguins by Jenny Markert. Child's World, 1999. (K–2) Describes the physical characteristics, behavior, habitat and life cycle of penguins. Great photos.

Gus & Gertie and the Lucky Charms by Joan Lowery Nixon. Sea Star Books, 2001. (2–3) Penguins Gus and Gertie take part in the Animals' Winter Olympics.

Penguin Chick by Betty Tatham. HarperCollins, 2002. (K–3) Follows the growth of one penguin chick from egg to adulthood. Part of the Let's-Read-and-Find-Out Science series.

Little Penguin's Tale by Audrey Wood. Scholastic, 1993. (PK–1) Searching for fun in his snowy polar world, Little Penguin dances with the gooney birds, cavorts at the Walrus Polar Club and narrowly escapes being eaten by a whale.

Act it Out

Try to walk like a penguin.

Standing Verse

Penguin walking all around,
(Walk like a penguin.)
Where have all the others gone?
(Hold hands up and look around.)
Turn around and touch the ground,
(Turn around and touch the ground.)
Then hurry back to penguin town.
(Waddle back to your seat.)

Penguin Tubey

Parts You'll Need

- Small Tube Cover (Black)
- Penguin Tummy (White)
- 2 Penguin Wings (Black)
- Penguin Beak (Orange)

Materials You'll Need

- half cardboard tube, 2¼ inches tall
- construction paper
- scissors
- glue
- single hole punch
- black marker

Directions

1. Cover the tube with the black tube cover. Overlap the ends and glue them together.

2. Glue the tummy just above the bottom of the tube.

3. Fold the wings along the fold line. Glue each folded end to one of the penguin's sides. The wings should hang down along the body.

4. Hole punch two white dots for the eyes and glue them on.

5. Use the black marker to draw pupils in the center of the eyes.

6. Fold the beak in half. Glue the bottom of the beak to the face so the beak is pointing down. Part of the beak will be glued to the tummy piece.

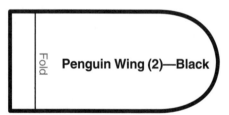

Penguin Wing (2)—Black

Penguin Beak—Orange

Penguin Tummy—White

Valentine's Day

Celebrate Valentine's Day with this heartwarming storytime.

Books to Enjoy

Sweet Hearts by Jan Carr. Holiday House, 2002. (PK–K) A little panda celebrates Valentine's Day by making and hiding paper hearts around the house for his family to discover. Includes directions for making hearts and a brief history of Valentine's Day.

The Runaway Valentine by Tina Casey. Albert Whitman & Co., 2001. (PK–2) Victor, a Valentine card, is eager to be brought home until he falls off the card display, marches out the door and becomes helpful to one person after another.

Today is Valentine's Day by P. K. Hallinan. Ideals Children's Books, 2001. (PK–1) A child describes Valentine's Day at school and the special cards the children give and receive.

A Mother for Choco by Keiko Kasza. Putnam, 1992. (PK–K) Although not about Valentine's Day, it is a story about love. A lonely little bird named Choco goes in search of a mother.

Danny's Mystery Valentine by Edith Kunhardt. Greenwillow Books, 1987. (PK–K) Danny and his mother go in search of the person who left Danny an unsigned valentine.

Froggy's First Kiss by Jonathan London. Viking, 1998. (PK–1) Froggy is excited about Valentine's Day and the new girl in class, until she gives him his first kiss.

One Zillion Valentines by Frank Modell. Trumpet Club, 1992. (PK–2) When Marvin shows Milton how to make valentines, they decide to make one for each person in their neighborhood.

Valentine's Day by Anne Rockwell. HarperCollins, 2001. (K–2) The children in Mrs. Madoff's class make special valentine cards to send to a friend in Japan and to share in their classroom celebration.

Set the Scene

Decorate with hearts of all sizes and red and white crepe paper streamers. Play birdcall sounds.

Poems

Roses are Red

Roses are red,
Violets are blue,
Sugar is sweet,
And so are you.

Little Birdie

Once a little birdie came hop, hop, hop.
I said, "Little birdie, won't you stop, stop, stop?"
I was going to the window to say, "How do you do?"
When he shook his little feathers and away he flew.

Fingerplays

Lovebirds

Two little lovebirds sitting in a tree,
(Hold up index finger of each hand.)
K-I-S-S-I-N-G.
(Fingers face each other and tap together to kiss.)
First comes love, then comes marriage,
(Make an 'X' with one side of fingers, then the other.)
Then comes the baby in a baby carriage.
(Hold arms and rock baby.)

Jack and Jill

Two little lovebirds sitting on a hill,
(Sit with knees up and perch one finger from each hand on the top of each knee.)
One named Jack and the other named Jill.
(Wiggle one finger for Jack and the other for Jill.)
Fly away Jack.
(Jack goes behind back.)
Fly away Jill.
(Jill goes behind back.)
Come back Jack.
(Jack comes back to knee.)
Come back Jill.
(Jill comes back to knee.)

If I Were a Bird

I wish I were a bird,
(Flutter hands at side of body.)
I'd fly up in the sky,
(Flutter hands up high.)
And see all the little people,
(Hold thumb and forefinger to show how little the people would look.)
When I look from way up high.
(Make eyeglasses at eyes and look down.)

Lovebird Tubey

Parts You'll Need

- Small Tube Cover (Red)
- Bird Head (Red)
- 2 Bird Wings and 1 Tail (Red)
- Bird Beak (Orange)

Materials You'll Need

- half cardboard tube, 2¼ inches tall
- construction paper
- scissors
- glue
- single hole punch
- black marker
- heart hole punch or heart stickers *(optional)*

Directions

1. Cover the tube with the red tube cover. Overlap the ends and glue them together.

2. Fold the beak in half and glue it to the middle of the face. The pointy end should be facing down.

3. Hole punch two brown dots for the eyes and glue them on. Use the marker to draw on pupils.

4. Glue the head to the top of the body.

5. Glue the tail inside the back of the tube so the feathers are sticking up.

6. Fold the end of each wing along the fold line. Glue each folded end to the inside of one of the bird's sides. The feathers should be sticking down. Slightly bend the wing and tail pieces after they dry.

7. If desired, add white heart hole punch decorations or small heart stickers.

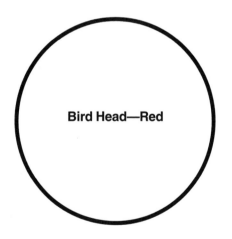

Bird Head—Red

Bird Wings (2) and Tail—Red

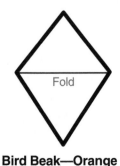

Bird Beak—Orange

Presidents' Day

Since 1971, the third Monday in February has celebrated Washington's Birthday. But the holiday has popularly become known as President's Day, a day for honoring Washington and Lincoln, who was also born in February, as well as all of the other presidents. Celebrate the holiday with a Presidents' Day storytime.

Books to Enjoy

Presidents' Day by Laura Alden. Children's Press, 1994. (PK–2) A teacher announces that there will be two famous guests visiting, Presidents Washington and Lincoln, and invites the class to ask questions about their lives. Also includes the legend of Washington and the cherry tree and the true story of Lincoln's beard.

A. Lincoln and Me by Louise Borden. Scholastic, 1999. (K–3) A boy who has the same birthday as Abe Lincoln discovers that he possesses some of the same characteristics and attributes as the great president.

Abraham Lincoln by Amy L. Cohn and Suzy Schmidt. Scholastic, 2002. (2–3) A simple biography of the Illinois lawyer who served the country as president through the difficulties of the Civil War.

If You Grew Up with George Washington by Ruth Belov Gross. Scholastic, 1993. (2–3) This is a great book to use as a basis for a discussion about what it was like to live in the time of George Washington.

George Washington by Cheryl Harness. National Geographic Society, 2000. (K–3) Presents the life of George Washington, focusing on the Revolutionary War and his presidency.

George Washington: Our First President by Garnet Jackson. Scholastic, 2000. (K–2) A simple biography of George Washington.

Presidents' Day by David F. Marx. Children's Press, 2002. (K–2) Discusses Presidents' Day and the significant achievements of the presidents it honors, George Washington and Abraham Lincoln.

Learning About Honesty from the Life of Abraham Lincoln by Kiki Mosher. PowerKids Press, 1996. (K–4) Extols the virtues of honesty through examples in the life of Abraham Lincoln.

Abraham Lincoln by Lucia Raatma. Compass Point Books, 2000. (1–3) A brief biography of the sixteenth president, known as a wise and compassionate man and an eloquent speaker, whose determination helped preserve the Union during the Civil War.

Abe Lincoln Remembers by Ann Warren Turner. HarperCollins, 2001. (1–3) Deeply moving text and large illustrations present Abe Lincoln's memories of his life.

When Abraham Talked to the Trees by Elizabeth Van Steenwyk. Eerdmans Books for Young Readers, 2000. (1–3) Abraham Lincoln's love for words—the reading, writing and speaking of them—began when he was young. Though his early years were filled with hardship and loss, he had a hunger for learning and persisted in his determination to develop the skills he would need later in his life.

Mr. Lincoln's Whiskers by Karen B. Winnick. Boyds Mills Press, 1996. (1–3) The true story of Grace Bedell, a child who wrote a letter to Abraham Lincoln, suggesting that he grow a beard.

Set the Scene

Play patriotic music and decorate the area with red, white and blue streamers, balloons and American flags. Display enlarged $1 and $5 bills, pennies and quarters so the likenesses of Washington and Lincoln can be seen.

Songs

Happy Birthday
Sing "Happy Birthday" to George and Abe.

My Hat it Has Three Corners
In honor of George Washington's hat.

My hat it has three corners.

Three corners has my hat.

And had it not three corners,

It would not be my hat.

Sing the song a few times, then tap your head instead of saying "hat" one time through.

Next time, tap your head for "hat" and hold up three fingers instead of saying "three."

The last round, tap your head, hold up three fingers and use your two index fingers to make a corner instead of saying "corner."

Game

Honest Abe

The players sit on the floor and one player goes to the front and turns his or her back. Then the players pass a penny until the player in the front says to stop. He or she turns and faces the others. The player has three chances to guess who is hiding the penny. "Honest Abe," the player holding the penny, must tell the truth if picked. Then Honest Abe becomes the player in the front.

George Washington Tubey

Parts You'll Need

- George's Pants (Gray)
- George's Coat (Black)
- George's Shirt (Blue)
- George's Hair (White)
- George's Collar (White)
- George's Hat (Black)
- George's Face (Peach)

Materials You'll Need

- cardboard tube, 4½ inches tall
- construction paper
- scissors
- glue
- black marker
- single hole punch
- pencil

Directions

1. Cover the bottom half of the tube with the gray pants. Overlap the ends and glue them together.

2. Glue the blue shirt on, just overlapping the pants.

3. Glue the face on the top half of the tube. Overlap the ends and glue them together.

4. Glue the collar over the top of the shirt seam.

5. Fold the coat along the fold lines. Glue the coat on so that it opens in the front.

6. Cut slits in the hair as indicated on the pattern. Glue the hair along the top edge of the tube. Use a pencil to curl the hair. Glue it up if necessary.

7. Hole punch two blue dots for the eyes and use the marker to draw on black pupils and a mouth. Glue the eyes on.

8. Fold the corners of the hat along the fold lines. Set the hat on George's head.

George's Pants—Gray

George's Face—Peach

George Washington Tubey (continued)

George's Collar—White

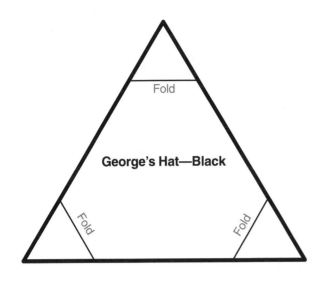

George's Hat—Black

George's Shirt—Blue

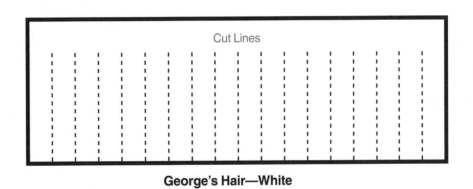

Cut Lines

George's Hair—White

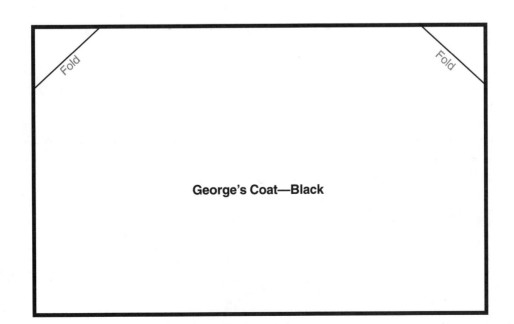

George's Coat—Black

Abraham Lincoln Tubey

Parts You'll Need

- Basic Tube Cover (Black)
- Basic Hat Pieces 1 and 2 (Black)
- Abe's Face (Peach)
- Abe's Beard (Black)
- Abe's Shirt (White)
- Abe's Bow Tie (Black)

Materials You'll Need

- cardboard tube, 4½ inches tall
- construction paper
- scissors
- glue
- black marker
- single hole punch

Directions

1. Cover the tube with the black tube cover. Overlap the ends and glue them together.

2. Center the face onto the beard and glue it in place.

3. Hole punch two blue dots for the eyes and glue them onto the face. Use the marker to draw on a nose and mouth.

4. Glue the beard and face to the top center of the tube.

5. Glue the white shirt right under the beard.

6. Glue the bow tie across the shirt.

7. Make the hat following the instructions on page 6. Place the hat on Abe's head.

Abe's Beard—Black

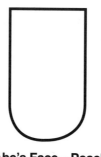

Abe's Face—Peach

Abe's Shirt—White

Abe's Bow Tie—Black

St. Patrick's Day

St. Patrick's Day celebrates St. Patrick, the patron saint of Ireland. The leprechaun, a mischievous elf that will reveal a hidden pot of gold if he is caught, is a symbol of St. Patrick's Day. Celebrate St. Patrick's Day with this storytime and Leprechaun Tubey.

Books to Enjoy

St. Patrick's Day by Gail Gibbons. Holiday House, 1994. (K–2) Simple text and colorful illustrations explain the story of St. Patrick. Includes six legends about St. Patrick.

Dear Old Donegal by Steve Graham. Clarion, 1996. (K–3) Through the rhyming verses of this song, an Irish immigrant to the United States relates his success in his new country and his delight at the prospect of going back to Ireland.

St. Patrick's Day: Parades, Shamrocks and Leprechauns by Elaine Landau. Enslow Publishers, Inc., 2002. (2–3) The story of St. Patrick's Day.

Jack and the Leprechaun by Ivan Robertson. Random House, 2000. (K–2) Jack the mouse visits his cousin in Ireland on St. Patrick's Day and tries to catch a leprechaun.

Clever Tom and the Leprechaun: An Old Irish Story by Linda Shute. Lothrop, Lee & Shepard Books, 1988. (K–5) Clever Tom Fitzpatrick thinks his fortune is made when he captures a leprechaun and forces him to reveal the hiding place of his gold, but the leprechaun is clever, too.

Poem

You Are Very, Very Lucky

You are very, very lucky,
If you catch a leprechaun.
You may see him picking shamrocks,
In your garden or your lawn.

If you catch him, he must give you,
All his treasure 'til it's gone!
You are very, very lucky,
If you catch a leprechaun.

Act it Out

Pretend you are looking all around for a leprechaun. What does he look like? Where is a good place for him to hide? When you see him, try to catch him. Oh, no! He slipped through your fingers! Better try again! Now where will you put him so he cannot get away?

Rainbows

Use rainbows as an additional theme. Let the children color a rainbow. Talk about rainbows. Make rainbows around the room by hanging many different colors of crepe paper streamers. At the end have a "pot of gold" filled with gold-wrapped candies or candy coins.

Leprechaun Tubey

Parts You'll Need

- Small Tube Cover (Green)
- Basic Hat Piece 1 (Light Green)
- Leprechaun's Hat Top (Light Green)
- Leprechaun's Hatband (Yellow)
- Leprechaun's Face (Peach)
- Leprechaun's Hair (Orange)
- Leprechaun's Vest (Light Green)
- Leprechaun's Bow Tie (Green)
- Leprechaun's Shamrock (Green) or Shamrock Sticker

Materials You'll Need

- half cardboard tube, 2¼ inches tall
- construction paper
- scissors
- glue
- black marker
- single hole punch
- shamrock sticker (optional)

Directions

1. Cover the tube with the green tube cover. Overlap the ends and glue them together.

2. Glue the leprechaun's face along the top edge of the tube.

3. Glue on the leprechaun's hair.

4. Glue on the light green vest.

5. Glue the bow tie to the top of the vest.

6. Hole punch two green dots for the eyes and use the marker to draw on pupils and a mouth. Glue on the eyes.

7. Make the hat following the instructions on page 6, using Basic Hat Piece 1 and the Leprechaun Hat Top.

8. Glue the hatband around the hat.

9. Glue or stick the shamrock to the front of the hatband. Set the hat on the leprechaun's head.

 Leprechaun's Bow Tie—Green

Leprechaun's Face—Peach

Leprechaun's Hair—Orange

Leprechaun Tubey (continued)

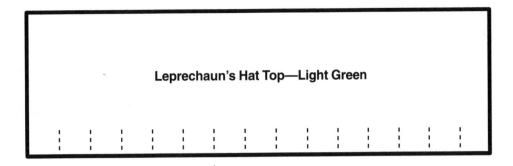

Leprechaun's Hat Top—Light Green

Leprechaun's Shamrock—Green

Leprechaun's Hatband—Yellow

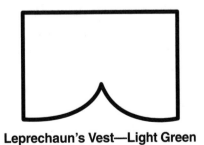

Leprechaun's Vest—Light Green

Easter

Easter is a time to celebrate the arrival of spring. Have fun with stories, fingerplays and the bunny hop. Then make Easter Bunny Tubeys.

Books to Enjoy

Humbug Rabbit by Lorna Balian. Abingdon Press, 1974. (PK–1) Father Rabbit's reply of "Humbug" to the idea that he is the Easter Rabbit doesn't spoil Easter for his children or Granny's grandchildren.

Easter Parade by Mary Chalmers. Harper & Row, 1988. (PK–1) The Easter animals gather for a springtime parade and Easter baskets.

The Easter Bunny that Overslept by Priscilla and Otto Friedrich. HarperCollins, 2002. (PK–2) Having slept past Easter, the Easter Bunny tries to distribute his eggs on Mother's Day, the Fourth of July and Halloween. At Christmastime, Santa gets him back on track.

Daddy Long Ears by Robert Kraus. Windmill Books/Simon & Schuster, 1982. (PK) As a single father of 31 bunnies, Daddy Long Ears (the Easter Bunny) does his best to care for his children and celebrate the holidays.

Easter Bunnies by Patrick Merrick. Child's World, 2000. (PK–2) Even the youngest audience will enjoy these large, colorful photographs of bunnies, colored eggs and Easter scenes that explain the origin of Easter traditions.

Happy Easter, Davy! by Brigitte Weninger. North-South Books, 2001. (PK–1) Davy the bunny decides to pose as the Easter Bunny when he thinks the bunny family will not get a visit from the real one.

Do the Bunny Hop!

Use the "Bunny Hop" song or sing it yourself. Have all of the little bunnies stand in a line or in a circle with everyone facing the same direction.

Put your right foot forward.
(Put right foot out and back two times.)
Put your left foot out.

(Put left foot out and back two times.)
Do the Bunny Hop!
(Jump forward once, jump back once.)
Hop! Hop! Hop!
(Jump forward three times.)

Repeat until song is over or until everyone is back to starting position.

Fingerplay

Funny Bunny

Here is a bunny with ears so funny,
(Hold up two fingers on right hand.)
And here is his home in the ground.
(Cup left hand.)
When a noise he hears, he pricks up his ears,
(Hold up right hand two fingers.)
And jumps into his home in the ground.
(Point two fingers down into left hand.)

Mirror Fingerplay

Start with two hands behind your back, folding your middle two fingers over your thumb (bunny nose) and holding your pointer and pinky fingers up (ears).

I'm a little bunny.
(Hop right-hand bunny around to front.)
He's a bunny, too.
(Hop left-hand bunny around to front.)
He does everything I do.
(Both bunnies look toward audience, then each other, then look at audience.)
I can wiggle my nose. *(Both thumbs wiggle.)*
I can wiggle my ears. *(Wiggle bunny ears.)*
I can hop, hop, hop.
(Both bunnies hop up and down.)
Hey! I'm looking in the mirror!
(Both bunnies look at each other, then at audience.)

Easter Bunny Tubey

Parts You'll Need

- Basic Tube Cover (Pink)
- Basic Hat Piece 1 (Purple)
- Bunny Hat Top (Purple)
- Bunny Hatband (Turquoise)
- Bunny Vest (Turquoise)
- Bunny Bow Tie (Purple)
- Bunny Ears (Pink)

Materials You'll Need

- cardboard tube, 4½ inches tall
- construction paper
- scissors
- single hole punch
- glue
- black marker

Directions

1. Cover the tube with the pink tube cover. Overlap the ends and glue them together.

2. Glue the turquoise vest to the bunny's front.

3. Glue the bow tie to the top of the vest.

4. Hole punch two purple dots for the vest buttons and glue them on.

5. Hole punch two turquoise dots for the eyes and one bright pink dot for the nose. Use the marker to draw on pupils and whiskers. Glue on the eyes and the nose.

6. Make the hat following the directions on page 6, using Basic Hat Piece 1 and the Bunny Hat Top.

7. Glue the hatband around the bottom of the hat.

8. Glue the bottom of the bunny ears to the inside front of the hat. The ears should stick up out of the hat.

9. Set the hat on the bunny's head.

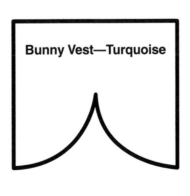

Bunny Vest—Turquoise

Bunny Bow Tie—Purple

Bunny Hat Top—Purple

Cut Lines

Bunny Hatband—Turquoise

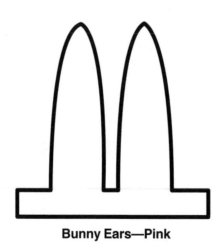

Bunny Ears—Pink

Butterflies

Butterflies are a sign of springtime. Use this storytime to celebrate the first day of spring or any other sunny spring day.

Books to Enjoy

What is a Butterfly? by Chris Arvetis. Children's Press, 1988. (PK–2) Introduces children to facts about caterpillars and butterflies.

The Very Hungry Caterpillar by Eric Carle. Philomel, 1987. (PK–2) A hungry little caterpillar eats a lot and becomes a big caterpillar. He spins a cocoon and soon emerges in a most delightful way.

Charlie the Caterpillar by Dom DeLuise. Simon & Schuster, 1990. (PK–2) A caterpillar is rejected by various groups of animals, until he grows his beautiful wings and is able to befriend a similarly unhappy caterpillar.

Clara Caterpillar by Pamela Duncan Edwards. HarperCollins, 2001. (1–3) By camouflaging herself, Clara Caterpillar, who becomes a cream-colored butterfly, courageously saves Catisha the crimson-colored butterfly from a hungry cow.

Waiting for Wings by Lois Ehlert. Harcourt, 2001. (PK–2) Follows the life cycle of four common butterflies, from their beginnings as tiny hidden eggs and hungry caterpillars to their transformation into full-grown butterflies.

Farfallina and Marcel by Holly Keller. Greenwillow Books, 2002. (PK–3) Once there was a caterpillar named Farfallina, whose best friend was a gosling named Marcel. They played together all the time. But one day everything changed.

The Caterpillar and the Polliwog by Jack Kent. Simon & Schuster, 1987. (PK–3) When the caterpillar tells the polliwog that she will turn into a beautiful butterfly when she grows up, polliwog decides to watch what she does very carefully so he can turn into a butterfly, too.

Angelina and the Butterfly by Sally-Ann Lever. Pleasant Company Publications, 2002. (PK–2) When Angelina the mouse finds a pink butterfly with a twisted leg, she's determined to look after it and keep it forever until a surprising turn of events sets the butterfly free.

The Butterfly Alphabet by Kjell Sandved. Scholastic, 1996. (PK–K) Find all the letters of the alphabet hiding in beautiful photographs of butterfly wing patterns.

Butterfly by Kim Taylor. Dorling Kindersley, Ltd., 1992. (PK–K) Lovely photographs and drawings trace the life cycle of a butterfly. Part of the See How They Grow series.

Fingerplay

Little Green Caterpillar

Little green caterpillar crawling in the sun,
(*Use right pointer finger to inch across left palm.*)
Little green caterpillar having lots of fun,
(*Use right pointer finger to inch across left palm.*)
Then he goes inside his house,
(*Put pointer finger inside left hand and close left hand.*)
And waves to us "bye-bye."
(*Keep left hand closed, wave with right hand.*)
And when he wakes up he will be,
A lovely butterfly.
(*Put right hand on top of left hand and flutter fingers to fly away.*)

Butterfly Tubey

Parts You'll Need

- Small Tube Cover (Black)
- Butterfly Head (Black)
- Butterfly Wings (Yellow)
- 4 Butterfly Wing Centers (Green and Purple)

Materials You'll Need

- half cardboard tube, 2¼ inches tall
- construction paper
- scissors
- glue
- single hole punch

Directions

1. Cover the tube with the black tube cover. Overlap the ends and glue them together.

2. Glue the wing centers onto the center of each wing section. The coordinating colors should be across from each other.

3. Glue the wings to the back of the tube.

4. Hole punch two green dots for eyes and glue them in place on the butterfly's head.

5. Glue the head to the front of the tube.

Variation: Make several butterflies with different colored wings for a colorful spring display.

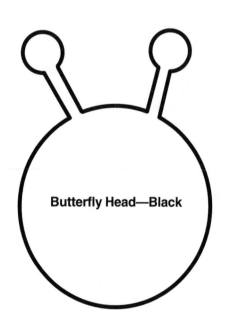

Butterfly Head—Black

Butterfly Tubey (continued)

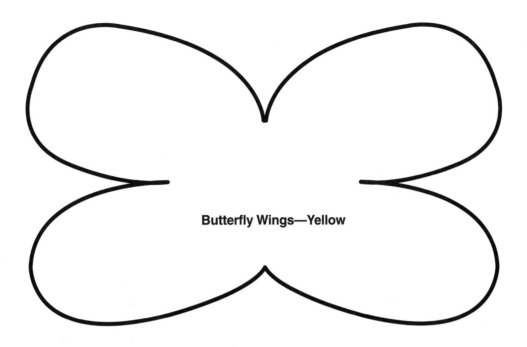

Butterfly Wings—Yellow

Butterfly Wing Centers—
(2) Green and (2) Purple

Lei Day

In Hawaii, Lei Day is May Day. The first Lei Day was held May 1, 1928. It is a day to celebrate Hawaii's state symbol of friendship and welcome. Events include state-wide lei competitions, the crowning of a Lei Queen and assorted exhibits and hula performances. This storytime lets you celebrate Lei Day wherever you live.

Books to Enjoy

"A" is for Aloha by Stephanie Feeney. University Press of Hawaii, 1980. (PK–K) Uses the ABC format to portray some of the people, places and events in the lives of children in Hawaii.

A Lei for Tutu by Rebecca Nevers Fellows. A. Whitman, 1998. (1–2) Nahoa loves making leis with her grandmother and looks forward to helping her create a special one for Lei Day, until her grandmother becomes very ill.

Luka's Quilt by Georgia Guback. Greenwillow Books, 1994. (PK–2) When Luka's grandmother makes her a traditional Hawaiian quilt, they disagree over the colors it should include.

Aloha Salty by Gloria Rand. Henry Holt, 1996. (PK–2) Zack and his dog Salty run into a bad storm while on a boat trip to Hawaii, but end up safe at a wonderful luau.

Aloha Dolores by Barbara Samuels. Dorling Kindersley, Ltd., 2000. (K–3) Certain that they will win a trip to Hawaii, Dolores enters her cat Duncan in the Meow Munchies contest and goes all out preparing for their trip.

Punia and the King of Sharks: A Hawaiian Folktale adapted by Lee Wardlaw. Dial, 1997. (1–3) This wonderfully illustrated story tells how Punia, a Hawaiian fisherman's son, tests his wits against the King of the Sharks.

Set the Scene

Decorate with colorful flowers, seashells, fish nets and Hawaiian travel posters. Play Hawaiian music as the children arrive.

Make Leis

Make leis before your storytime, or let the children make them as part of the program.

Materials you will need:

- Different colors of tissue paper

- Plastic drinking straws cut into 1-inch lengths

- Yarn or string cut into 30-inch lengths

Use the pattern below to cut out different colors of flowers from tissue paper. Hole punch the center of each flower. Knot one end of a piece of yarn. Thread three flowers onto the yarn, then one piece of straw. Continue until the yarn is full. Tie off the ends and wear!

Flower Pattern

Tell a Story

Try these simple hand gestures to tell the story of a "Hukilau." Hukilau is a Hawaiian custom where people throw large nets into the ocean, chase fish into them, then pull the nets in. Finally, the Hawaiians cook the fish and have a feast called a luau.

Sit on the floor and perform the following hand gestures:

Oh, we're going,
(*Put your left hand on your left hip, then with your right hand gesture over your shoulder with your right thumb in a hitchhike motion.*)
To the hukilau.
(*Pull hands towards you as if pulling in a fishing net.*)
Everybody loves,
(*At front of body, cross both wrists with hands facing each other and wave fingers softly.*)
The hukilau. (*Pull the nets in again.*)

Where the lau-lau, (fish)
(*Place your right hand on top of your left hand, both hands with palms down and fingers to front, then wiggle thumbs to show fish fins.*)
Is the kau-kau, (food)
(*Turn your left palm up, take two fingers from your right hand and tap your left palm, then the two fingers draw a circle around your mouth.*)
At the big luau. (party)
(*Both hands open overhead and down to the sides.*)

Snack

Serve pieces of fruit on toothpicks for a tropical snack.

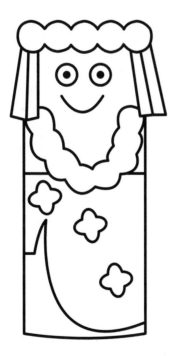

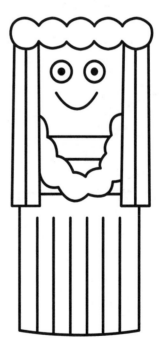

Hawaiian Boy Tubey

Parts You'll Need

- Basic Tube Cover (Brown)
- Hawaiian Boy's Pareu (Red)
- Hawaiian Boy's Head Wreath (Yellow)
- Hawaiian Boy's Lei (Yellow)
- 6 Hawaiian Boy's Pareu Decorations (Yellow)
- Hawaiian Boy's Hair (Black)

Materials You'll Need

- cardboard tube, 4½ inches tall
- construction paper
- scissors
- glue
- black marker
- single hole punch

Directions

1. Cover the tube with the brown tube cover. Overlap the ends and glue them together.

2. Glue on the red pareu so the slit is at the side of the tube.

3. Cut slits in the hair as indicated on the pattern. Glue the hair along the top edge of the tube.

4. Glue the head wreath around the top edge of the tube.

5. Glue on the lei so it just overlaps the pareu.

6. Glue the decorations on the pareu.

7. Hole punch two brown dots for the eyes and use the marker to draw on black pupils and a mouth. Glue on the eyes.

Lei—Yellow (Boy) or Red (Girl)

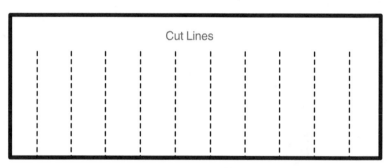

Hawaiian Boy's Hair—Black

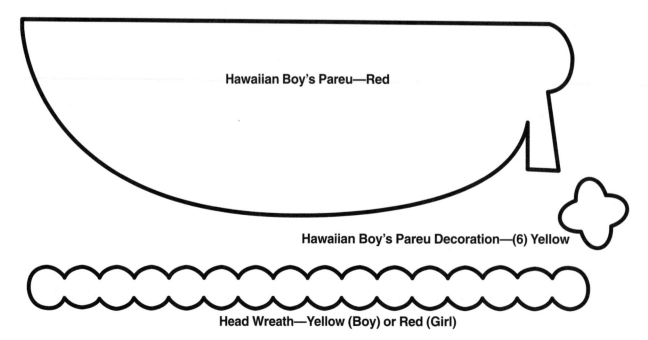

Hawaiian Boy's Pareu—Red

Hawaiian Boy's Pareu Decoration—(6) Yellow

Head Wreath—Yellow (Boy) or Red (Girl)

Hawaiian Girl Tubey

Parts You'll Need

- Basic Tube Cover (Brown)
- Hawaiian Girl's Skirt (Green)
- Hawaiian Girl's Top (Yellow)
- Hawaiian Girl's Hair (Black)
- Hawaiian Girl's Lei (Red)—pg. 32
- Hawaiian Girl's Head Wreath (Red)—pg. 32

Materials You'll Need

- cardboard tube, 4½ inches tall
- construction paper
- scissors
- glue
- black marker
- single hole punch

Directions

1. Cover the tube with the brown tube cover. Overlap the ends and glue them together.

2. Cut slits in the skirt as indicated on the pattern. Glue on the skirt along the bottom edge of the tube.

3. Glue on the yellow top.

4. Cut slits in hair as indicated on pattern. Glue the hair along the top edge of the tube.

5. Glue the head wreath around the top edge of the tube.

6. Glue on the lei.

7. Hole punch two brown dots for the eyes and use the marker to draw on black pupils and a mouth. Glue on the eyes.

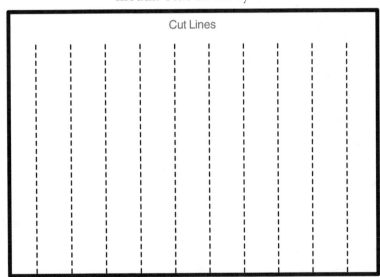

Hawaiian Girl's Top—Yellow

Hawaiian Girl's Hair—Black

Cut Lines

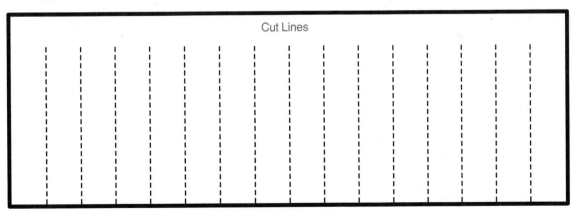

Cut Lines

Hawaiian Girl's Skirt—Green

Cinco de Mayo

Cinco de Mayo, or the "Fifth of May," celebrates Mexico's victory over a larger and more powerful army during a battle in 1862. The holiday celebrates Mexico's freedom and liberty. Cinco de Mayo is celebrated in Mexico and in many cities in the United States. Take a short vacation to Mexico for this fun storytime.

Books to Enjoy

How Nanita Learned to Make Flan by Campbell Geeslin. Atheneum Books, 1999. (K–3) The cobbler in a Mexican town is so busy that he cannot make shoes for his daughter. One night she makes her own shoes, which take her far away. Includes a recipe for flan.

In Rosa's Mexico by Campbell Geeslin. Random House, 1996. (PK–K) Three stories about a Mexican girl's encounters with a rooster, a burro and a wolf. Each story uses some Spanish words that are defined at the beginning of the book.

The Moon Was at a Fiesta by Matthew Gollub. Tortuga Press, 1997. (K–3) Jealous of the sun, the moon decides to create her own fiesta and celebrates a bit too much.

Hooray! A Piñata! by Elisa Kleven. Dutton Children's Books, 1996. (PK–2) After choosing a cute dog piñata for her birthday party, Clara pretends it is her pet and decides she does not want to break it. Includes the history of the piñata.

Fiestas: Holiday Songs from Latin America by José Luis Orozco. Penguin Putnam Books for Young Readers, 2002. (PK–3) Over 20 holiday songs and rhymes gathered from Spanish-speaking countries. Includes Cinco de Mayo.

Cinco de Mayo by Janet Riehecky. Children's Press, 1993. (PK–K) Although Maria is not too successful at helping her family prepare for Cinco de Mayo, she wins an art contest at the library and gets to break the piñata back home. Includes instructions for making tacos and crafts.

Mice and Beans by Pam Muñoz Ryan. Scholastic, 2001. (PK–2) In this rhythmic cumulative tale, Rosa Maria spends the week getting ready for her granddaughter's birthday party and trying to avoid attracting mice—unaware that the mice in her walls are preparing a party of their own.

Cinco de Mayo by Lola M. Schaefer. Pebble Books, 2001. (K–2) Very simple text and color photographs describe the celebration of Cinco de Mayo. Includes Cinco de Mayo Web sites.

Set the Scene

Play Mexican patriotic songs or other festive songs, decorate with red, white and green, set out colorful flowers and hang up small piñatas decorated with crepe paper streamers.

Song

Piñata!
(Sung to the tune: "Sing a Song of Sixpence")

Here is our piñata,
What a sight to see.
Filled with treats and goodies,
Just for you and me.
When it's time to break it,
We'll circle all around.
Then we'll scramble for the treats,
That fall down to the ground.

Mexican Hat Dance

Play the "Mexican Hat Dance" or another festive song from Mexico, or just do the following steps:

- Place a large hat (real or imaginary) on the floor.

- Have everyone stand in a circle facing the hat. Place your hands on your hips.

- Alternate feet out in front: Right, Left, Right, then clap your hands two times.

- Alternate feet out in front: Left, Right, Left, Clap, Clap.

- Alternate feet again: Right, Left, Right, Clap, Clap.

- Alternate feet again: Left, Right, Left, Clap, Clap.

- Then each player links arms with a partner and makes a circle in one direction, then in the other direction.

- Continue as the music suggests.

Mexican Boy Tubey

Parts You'll Need

- Basic Tube Cover (Tan)
- Mexican Boy's Hair (Black)
- Mexican Boy's Neckerchief (Red)
- Mexican Boy's Shirt (White)
- Mexican Boy's Pants (Blue)
- Serape Stripes (Red)
- 3 Serape Tassels (Gray)
- Mexican Boy's Serape (Gray)
- Mexican Boy's Hat Top (Yellow)
- Mexican Boy's Hat Brim (Yellow)

Materials You'll Need

- cardboard tube, 4½ inches tall
- construction paper
- scissors
- glue
- black marker
- single hole punch
- pencil

Directions

1. Cover the tube with the tan tube cover. Overlap the ends and glue them together.

2. Glue on the hair so that the curved edges are in the front.

3. Glue the white shirt just underneath the hair.

4. Glue on the blue pants.

5. Glue the red neckerchief along the top of the shirt.

6. Cut apart the serape stripes and glue them to the serape.

7. Glue the serape over the boy's shoulder. The angled edge should be at the shoulder. Then glue the tassels to the bottom.

8. Fold the hat top along the fold line. Glue the folded edge to the center of the hat brim.

9. Use a pencil to roll the hat brim up a little at the front edge.

10. Hole punch two brown dots for the eyes and use the marker to draw on black pupils and a mouth. Glue on the eyes.

Mexican Boy's Hair—Black

Mexican Boy's Neckerchief—Red

Mexican Boy Tubey (continued)

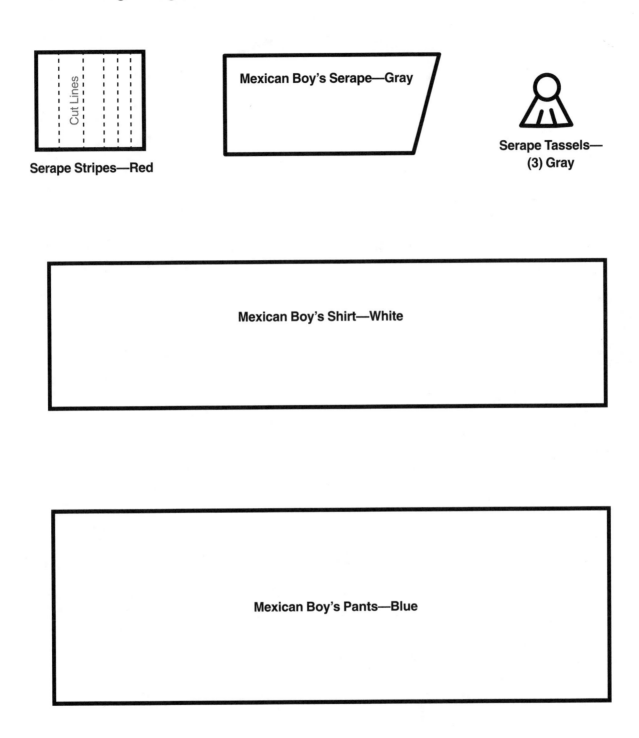

Cut Lines

Serape Stripes—Red

Mexican Boy's Serape—Gray

Serape Tassels—
(3) Gray

Mexican Boy's Shirt—White

Mexican Boy's Pants—Blue

Mexican Boy Tubey (continued)

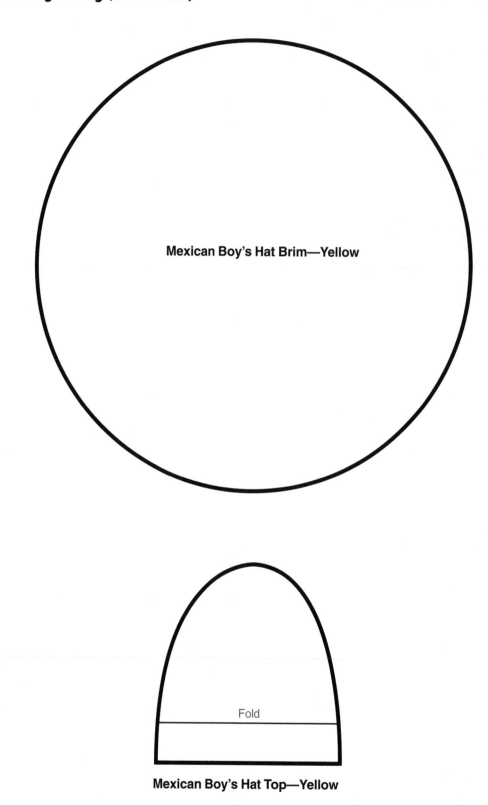

Mexican Boy's Hat Brim—Yellow

Fold

Mexican Boy's Hat Top—Yellow

Mexican Girl Tubey

Parts You'll Need

- Basic Tube Cover (Tan)
- Mexican Girl's Hair (Black)
- Mexican Girl's Vest (Blue)
- Mexican Girl's Blouse (Yellow)
- 8 Decorative Flowers (Red)

Materials You'll Need

- cardboard tube, 4½ inches tall
- construction paper
- scissors
- glue
- black marker
- single hole punch

Directions

1. Cover the tube with the tan tube cover. Overlap the ends and glue them together.

2. Glue on the yellow blouse.

3. Glue the blue vest over the yellow blouse so it closes in the front. Use one tan hole punch for the button.

4. Glue the hair on so the points meet in the front.

5. Glue flowers in the girl's hair and on her skirt.

6. Hole punch two brown dots for the eyes. Use the marker to draw on black pupils and a mouth. Glue on the eyes.

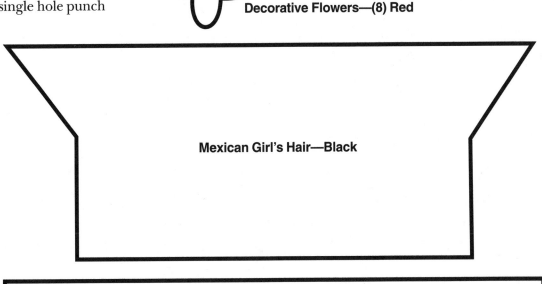

Decorative Flowers—(8) Red

Mexican Girl's Hair—Black

Mexican Girl's Blouse—Yellow

Mexican Girl's Vest—Blue

Frogs

June is Zoo and Aquarium Month. Visit an imaginary aquarium with this frog storytime.

Books to Enjoy

The Frog Principal by Stephanie Calmenson. Scholastic, 2001. (K–3) After a magician turns the principal of P.S. 88 into a frog, the frog bargains for the chance to act as principal until Mr. Bundy returns from his family emergency.

The Wide-Mouthed Frog by Keith Faulkner. Dial, 1996. (K–3) A wide-mouthed frog asks the advice of the other animals in the swamp about a proper diet. Then he meets an alligator who eats only wide-mouthed frogs.

Why Frogs Are Wet by Judy Hawes. HarperCollins, 2001. (K–3) Frogs can jump 30 times their own body length, catch insects on their tongue and breathe underwater or on land. But why must they always keep their skin wet?

Jump Frog Jump by Robert Kalan. Greenwillow Books, 1995. (PK—2) A fun tale about a frog who tries to catch a fly without getting caught himself. The children will enjoy calling out "Jump, Frog, Jump!"

Grandpa Toad's Secrets by Keiko Kasza. Putnam, 1995. (PK–K) Grandpa Toad teaches his grandson the secrets of survival, but Little Toad is the one who saves the day when a huge monster attacks them.

I Took My Frog to the Library by Eric A. Kimmel. Puffin Books, 1992. (K–2) A young girl brings her various pets to the library, with predictably disastrous results.

Froggy series by Jonathan London. Viking. (PK) Froggy learns many things in this hilarious series which includes baking a cake, eating out, getting dressed, going to school, etc.

Set the Scene

Play jungle or swamp sounds that have croaking frogs. Set out various frog stuffed animals. Display nonfiction books about frogs from your collection.

Fingerplays

Five Little Speckled Frogs

Five little speckled frogs,
(Show five fingers.)
Sitting on a speckled log.
(Set five fingers on top of the back of the other hand.)
Eating their very favorite bugs. Yum! Yum!
(Rub tummy.)

One jumped into the pond,
(One finger dives down.)
Where he swam round and round.
(Make swimming motions with arms.)
Now there are four speckled frogs.
(Show four fingers.)

(Continue counting down until there are …)
No speckled frogs. Boo Hoo!
(Rub eyes as if crying.)

Little Green Tadpole

Little green tadpole swimming all around,
(Make swimming motions.)
Little green tadpole can't hop on the ground.
(Try to hop but keep both feet on the ground.)
Soon your legs will start to grow,
(Point to legs.)
You will have a heel and toe,
(Point to heel and toe.)
You will be a green frog hopping all around.
(Hop around.)

Frog Tubey

Parts You'll Need

- Small Tube Cover (Green)
- Frog Face (Green)
- 2 Frog Legs (Green)

Materials You'll Need

- half cardboard tube, 2¼ inches tall.
- construction paper
- glue
- black marker
- single hole punch

Directions

1. Cover the tube with the green tube cover. Overlap the ends and glue them together.

2. Hole punch two black dots for the pupils. Glue the pupils on the frog's face. Use the marker to draw circles around the pupils and a mouth.

3. Glue the face to the front of the body.

4. Fold the legs along the fold lines. Glue each folded edge to one of the frog's sides.

5. Hole punch six light green dots and glue them to the legs.

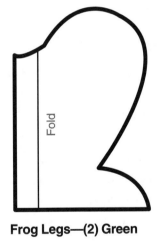

Frog Legs—(2) Green

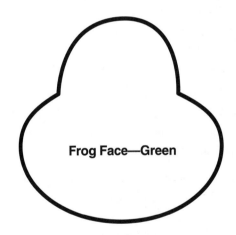

Frog Face—Green

Snakes

Show children how friendly snakes can be with fun stories, play action and snake tubeys.

Books to Enjoy

Hide and Snake by Keith Baker. Harcourt Brace Jovanovich, 1991. (PK–3) A brightly colored snake hides among colorful objects on each page. Can you find him?

Small Green Snake by Libba Moore Gray. Orchard Books, 1997. (PK–1) Despite his mother's warning not to wander, Small Green Snake wiggles away to investigate a new sound he hears coming from the other side of the garden wall.

I Need a Snake by Lynne Jonell. Penguin Putnam Books for Young Readers, 2000. (PK–2) A young boy really wants a snake of his own, and after his mother reads a book about snakes and takes him to a museum and a pet store to see some, he finds his own pet "snakes" around the house.

The Snake that Sneezed by Robert Leydenfrost. Putnam, 1970. (K–2) Harold the snake swallows every creature in sight, but gains fame and fortune when he has to sneeze at the circus.

The Day Jimmy's Boa Ate the Wash by Trinka Hakes Noble. Dial Books for Young Readers, 1980. (K–1) Jimmy's pet boa constrictor disrupts the class outing to the farm.

Jimmy's Boa Bounces Back by Trinka Hakes Noble. Dial Books for Young Readers, 1984. (K–3) Jimmy's pet boa constrictor wreaks havoc on a posh garden party.

Slinky, Scaly, Slithery Snakes by Dorothy Hinshaw Patent. Walker & Co., 2000. (2–3) Describes a variety of snakes including their unusual characteristics, habitats and behaviors.

Never Fear, Snake My Dear! by Rolf Siegenthaler. North-South Books, 2001. (K–2) A mouse intended to be dinner for a snake at the zoo digs a tunnel so that they can both escape to freedom, after which they share an unlikely friendship.

Crictor by Tomi Ungerer. Harper & Row, 1983. (PK–3) In a little French village, Madame Bodot receives an unexpected gift in a big round box. The pet snake soon becomes a town hero.

Set the Scene

Have someone from a local pet store bring in a snake for show and tell.

Act it Out

(Point to each body part as it is mentioned.)
I'm being swallowed by a boa constrictor!
Oh no! He swallowed my toe!
Oh gee! He swallowed my knee!
Oh my! He swallowed my thigh!
Oh fiddle! He swallowed my middle!
Oh heck! He swallowed my neck!
Oh dread! He swallowed my MMMMPHH!

Poem

A Snake

A snake is long and might be fun,
But if I see one, I will run!

Snake Tubey

Parts You'll Need

- Small Tube Cover (Green)
- Snake Head (Green)
- Snake Body (Green)
- Snake Tongue (Red)

Materials You'll Need

- half cardboard tube, 2¼ inches tall
- construction paper
- scissors
- glue
- single hole punch

Directions

1. Cover the tube with the green tube cover. Overlap the ends and glue them together.

2. Glue the edge of the tongue to the bottom of the head so the tongue sticks out.

3. Glue the snake's head to the square end of the body.

4. Hole punch two yellow dots for the eyes and eight light green dots for the decorations. Glue the eyes onto the head.

5. Cut eight pieces of yellow paper about ¾-inch long and ¼-inch wide to place between the light green dots.

6. Glue the yellow strips and the light green dots on the body in an alternating pattern.

7. Coil the snake's body around the tube and glue it in place.

Note: *After cutting out the head and body patterns, staple them together and cut out the green construction paper in one piece. This eliminates Step 3.*

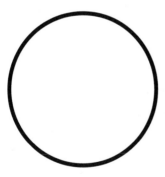

Snake Head—Green

Snake Tongue—Red

Snake Tubey (continued)

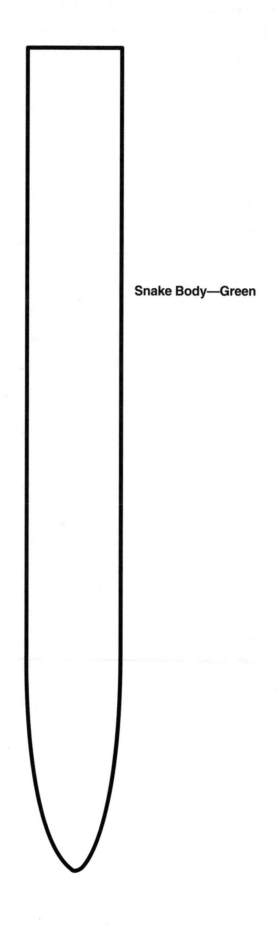

Snake Body—Green

Fourth of July

Independence Day commemorates the adoption of the Declaration of Independence in 1776. Celebrate the birthday of the United States with this patriotic storytime.

Books to Enjoy

Happy Birthday, America! by Marsha Wilson Chall. Lothrop, Lee & Shepard Books, 2000. (K–2) Joined by an army of aunts, uncles and cousins, eight-year-old Kay and her family celebrate the Fourth of July.

Henry's Fourth of July by Holly Keller. Greenwillow Books, 1985. (PK–K) Henry has fun enjoying the Fourth of July festivities with his family and friends.

Fourth of July by Janet McDonnell. Children's Press, 1994. (1–3) Nina and her dog Sammy enjoy the Fourth of July until Sammy chases a cat at the parade. Includes fireworks safety tips.

Hurray for the Fourth of July by Wendy Watson. Clarion Books, 1992. (PK–2) A small-town family celebrates the Fourth of July by attending a parade, having a picnic and watching fireworks. Includes traditional patriotic songs and rhymes.

Apple Pie 4th of July by Janet S. Wong. Harcourt, 2002. (PK–2) A Chinese American child fears that the food her parents are preparing to sell on the Fourth of July will not be eaten.

Hats Off for the Fourth of July by Harriet Ziefert. Viking, 2000. (PK–2) Spectators wait to see what will come next as they watch the town's Fourth of July parade.

Set the Scene

Play patriotic music, march around the room, decorate with flags and red, white and blue streamers and display an "Uncle Sam Wants You" poster.

Patriotic Songs

Happy Birthday

Sing "Happy Birthday" to the U.S.A.!

Yankee Doodle

Yankee Doodle went to town,
Riding on a pony.
He stuck a feather in his cap,
And called it macaroni.

Yankee Doodle keep it up,
Yankee Doodle dandy.
Mind the music and the step,
And with the girls be handy.

Yankee Doodle Dandy

I'm a Yankee Doodle Dandy,
Yankee Doodle do or die.
A real live nephew of my Uncle Sam,
Born on the Fourth of July.

You're my Yankee Doodle sweetheart,
I'm your Yankee Doodle toy.
Yankee Doodle went to London,
Just to ride a pony,
I am that Yankee Doodle boy!

Uncle Sam Tubey

Parts You'll Need

- Basic Tube Cover (White)
- Basic Hat Pieces 1 and 2 (White)
- Uncle Sam's Face (Peach)
- Uncle Sam's Goatee (White)
- Uncle Sam's Frock Coat (Blue)
- Uncle Sam's Stripes (Red)
- Uncle Sam's Stars (White)
- Uncle Sam's Hatband (Blue)

Materials You'll Need

- cardboard tube, 4½ inches tall
- construction paper
- scissors
- glue
- black marker
- single hole punch

Directions

1. Cover the tube with the white tube cover. Overlap the ends and glue them together.

2. Glue the face to the front of the tube along the top edge.

3. Cut the stripes along the lines, then glue four stripes to the front of the tube, along the bottom edge.

4. Glue on the frock coat so it opens in the front.

5. Glue on the goatee.

6. Hole punch two blue dots for the eyes. Use a marker to draw on black pupils, a nose and a mouth. Glue on the eyes.

7. Make the hat following the directions on page 6.

8. Glue six stripes to the hat. Trim the stripes at the top to fit.

9. Glue stars on the hatband.

10. Glue the hatband around the hat. Set the hat on Uncle Sam's head.

Uncle Sam's Stars—White

Uncle Sam's Goatee—White

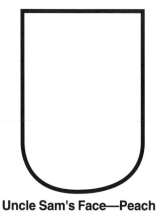

Uncle Sam's Face—Peach

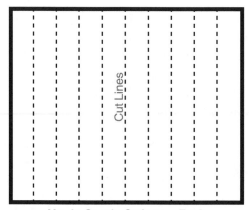

Uncle Sam's Stripes—Red

Cut Lines

Uncle Sam's Hatband—Blue

Uncle Sam Tubey (continued)

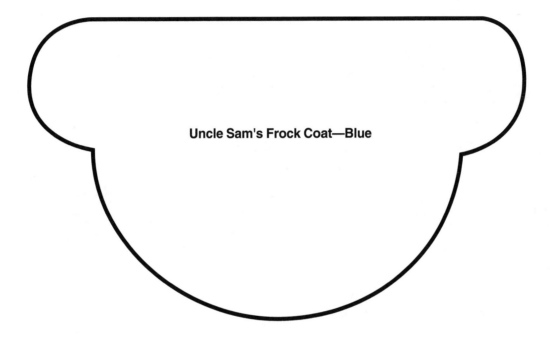

Uncle Sam's Frock Coat—Blue

Fish

Spend the hot days of August at the sea with this fishy storytime.

Books to Enjoy

Big Al by Andrew Clements. Picture Book Studio, 1988. (PK–2) A big ugly fish has trouble making friends because of his appearance until he saves them all from a fisherman's net.

Hello Fish! Visiting the Coral Reef by Sylvia A. Earle. National Geographic Society, 2001. (PK–3) An underwater explorer takes a tour of the ocean and introduces different fish.

Fish Eyes: A Book You Can Count On by Lois Ehlert. Harcourt, 2001. (PK–K) Wonderfully colorful fish counting book.

Fish is Fish by Leo Lionni. Alfred A. Knopf, 1970. (K–3) When his friend the tadpole becomes a frog and leaves the pond to explore the world, a little fish decides maybe he can leave the pond, too.

Swimmy by Leo Lionni. Scholastic, 1989. (PK–K) A small black fish in a school of small red fish figures out a way they can work together to protect themselves from the big predators.

Rainbow Fish by Marcus Pfister. North-South Books, 1992. (PK–1) The most beautiful fish in the ocean discovers the real value of friendship.

Rainbow Fish and the Sea Monsters' Cave by Marcus Pfister. North-South Books, 2001. (PK–1) In order to find healing algae for the ailing bumpy-backed fish, Rainbow Fish volunteers to brave the dreaded Sea Monsters' Cave.

One Fish, Two Fish, Red Fish, Blue Fish by Dr. Seuss. Random House, 1960. (1–2) A story-poem about the activities of a group of unusual animals.

Set the Scene

Play sounds of ocean waves and hang blue streamers from the ceiling. Have someone bring a small fish to share or ask someone from a local pet store to come and talk about the care of fish.

Act it Out

Pretend to wiggle your fins and swim. Pucker up to make fish sounds.

Go Fish!

Set up an area for "Go Fish!" Make a fishing pole out of a stick with a string tied to one end. Have the children cast the pole over a counter. Someone should be crouching down behind the counter so he or she can attach small gifts to the line, then jerk on the line to let the child know he or she has caught a fish.

Fingerplay

Five Little Fishes

(Hold up fingers as you count down.)

Five little fishes swimming near the shore.
One took a dive and then there were four.
Four little fishes were swimming out to sea.
One went for food and then there were three.
Three little fishes said, "Now what do we do?"
One swam away and then there were two.
Two little fishes were having great fun.
One took a plunge and then there was one.
One little fish said, "I like the warm sun."
Away she went and then there were none!

Fish Tubey

Parts You'll Need

- Small Tube Cover (Blue)
- Fish Tail (Lavender)
- 3 Fish Fins (Lavender)

Materials You'll Need

- half cardboard tube, 2¼ inches tall
- construction paper
- scissors
- glue
- single hole punch
- black marker
- small heart punch (*optional*)

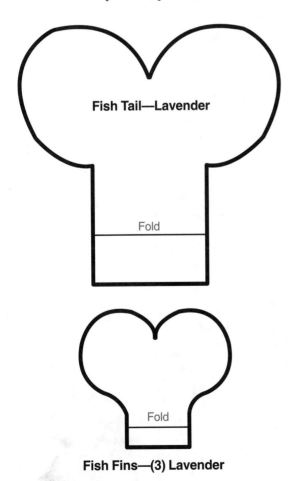

Fish Tail—Lavender

Fold

Fold

Fish Fins—(3) Lavender

Directions

1. Cover the tube with the blue tube cover. Overlap the ends and glue them together.

2. Fold the tail along the fold line. Glue the folded edge to the back of the tube, aligning it with the bottom edge. The tail should be perpendicular to the tube.

3. Fold the side fins along the fold lines. Glue one of the folded edges to each side of the fish.

4. Glue the last fin to the inside of the tube in the front. There should be about ½ inch of the fin sticking up out of the tube.

5. Use two lavender hole punch dots for the eyes. Use the marker to draw black pupils on the eyes. Glue them on. Use one red heart punch for the mouth or draw on a mouth.

6. If you wish, add blue hole punch dots to decorate the fins.

Note: *You can use any color of paper you wish. You might want to make your fish the same color as a fish from one of the stories. If you read* One Fish, Two Fish, Red Fish, Blue Fish *make your fish red and blue. Or for* Swimmy, *make one black fish and many red fish and act out the story.*

Mermaids

Your children will love this fantastic mermaid storytime.

Books to Enjoy

The Little Mermaid by Hans Christian Andersen, adapted by Rachel Isadora. Putnam, 1998. (K–3) A mermaid who longs to be human trades her tail for legs, hoping to win the love of a prince.

The Case of the Mysterious Mermaid by Vivian Binnamin. Silver Press, 1990. (K–3) Miss Whimsy's students search for a missing mermaid.

Babar and Zephir by Jean de Brunhoff. Random House, 2002. (K–2) Babar's monkey friend Zephir goes fishing and accidentally catches a mermaid. He enlists her aid in saving Princess Isabelle, who was kidnapped by a monster.

The Trouble with Uncle by Babette Cole. Little, Brown, 1992. (PK–3) Uncle, who is a pirate, starts his own club, buys a treasure map and marries a mermaid.

The Mermaid's Purse by Ted Hughes. Knopf, 2000. (3) Twenty-eight poems capture the beauty, drama and mystery of the sea and seashore.

Princess Fishtail by Frances Minters. Viking Penguin, 2002. (PK–2) Princess Fishtail digs her life beneath the water, then she rescues a handsome surfer and is hooked by love.

Set the Scene

Decorate with blue crepe paper, hang fish and starfish shapes around the room and cover the floor with blue balloons. Play the soundtrack to *The Little Mermaid*.

Poem

Five Little Sea Creatures

Five little sea creatures,
On the ocean floor;
The lobster walked away,
Now there are four.

Four little sea creatures,
Living in the sea;
The octopus crept away,
Now there are three.

Three little sea creatures,
Wondering what to do;
"Good-bye," said the starfish,
Now there are two.

Two little sea creatures,
Not having much fun;
Off swam the sea horse,
Now there is one.

One little mermaid,
Sad and all alone.
Back came the starfish,
Back came the sea horse,
Back came the octopus,
Back came the lobster,
Then all five went home.

Mermaid Tubey

Parts You'll Need

- Basic Tube Cover (Peach)
- Mermaid's Tail (Turquoise)
- Mermaid's Lower Body (Turquoise)
- Mermaid's Swim Top (Turquoise)
- Mermaid's Scales (12 each of Yellow, Blue and Purple)
- Mermaid's Hair (Brown)
- Mermaid's Headband (Turquoise)

Materials You'll Need

- cardboard tube, 4½ inches tall
- construction paper
- scissors
- glue
- star hole punch
- single hole punch
- black marker

Directions

1. Cover the tube with the peach tube cover. Overlap the ends and glue them together.

2. Glue the lower body along the bottom edge of the tube.

3. Glue on the swim top a little above the lower body.

4. Starting at the bottom of the lower body, glue on the scales. Each row should slightly overlap the previous row. Alternate the colors.

5. Glue more scales to the front of the tail, leaving a small turquoise border around the edge of the tail. Alternate the colors.

6. Fold the tail along the fold line. Glue the folded edge to the side of the lower body. Be careful to position the tail so the bottom fin is even with the bottom of the tube or it will not stand up.

7. Cut slits in the hair as indicated on the pattern. Glue the hair along the top edge of the tube.

8. Glue the headband over the hair, along the top edge of the tube.

9. Hole punch six yellow stars. Glue two on the swim top front and four on the headband.

10. Hole punch two turquoise dots for the eyes and use the marker to draw on black pupils and a mouth. Glue the eyes on.

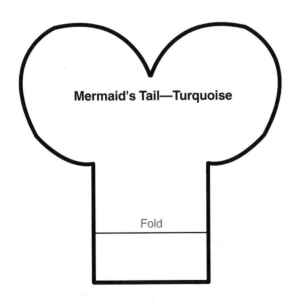

Mermaid's Tail—Turquoise

Fold

Mermaid Tubey (continued)

Mermaid's Hair—Brown

Cut Lines

**Mermaid's Scales—
(12 each)
Yellow, Purple and Blue**

Mermaid's Headband—Turquoise

Mermaid's Lower Body—Turquoise

Mermaid's Swim Top—Turquoise

Dogs

The dog days of summer are usually the hottest and muggiest of the year. Keep cool this August with a fun storytime about dogs.

Books to Enjoy

The Adventures of Taxi Dog by Debra and Sal Barracca. Puffin, 2000. (PK–2) A stray dog in New York City is adopted by a taxi driver. They share new adventures in the taxi each day.

Go, Dog, Go by P. D. Eastman. Random House, 1961. (PK–2) Dogs in all shapes, sizes and colors star in this wonderfully goofy book.

Dashing Dog by Margaret Mahy. Greenwillow Books, 2002. (PK–1) A dashing, daredevil dog is twirled around, ruffled and scuffled and wobbled and whirled around town.

Dog Days: Rhymes Around the Year by Jack Prelutsky. Knopf, 1999. (PK–2) A spirited dog describes what he enjoys doing each month of the year.

Officer Buckle and Gloria by Peggy Rathmann. Putnam, 1995. (K–3) The children at Naperville Elementary School always ignore Officer Buckle's safety tips, until a police dog named Gloria accompanies him when he gives his safety speeches. 1996 Caldecott Medal winner.

The Great Gracie Chase: Stop that Dog! by Cynthia Rylant. Blue Sky Press, 2001. (PK–1) Gracie has been a good dog every single day of her life, until some noisy painters arrive.

The Stray Dog by Marc Simont. HarperCollins, 2001. (K–3) The story of a picnicking family charmed by a stray dog.

Dear Mrs. LaRue: Letters from Obedience School by Mark Teague. Scholastic, 2002. (K–3) Gertrude LaRue receives typewritten and paw-written letters from her dog Ike, entreating her to let him leave the Igor Brotweiler Canine Academy and come back home.

Harry the Dirty Dog by Gene Zion. HarperCollins, 1956. (PK–2) More than anything else, Harry the dog hates baths. So he runs away from home and has the time of his life. But when he comes back at the end of the day, no one recognizes him because he's covered with dirt.

Fingerplay

Five Little Puppies

Five little puppies were playing in the sun.
(*Hold up one hand with your fingers extended.*)
This one saw a rabbit and he began to run.
(*Bend down first finger.*)
This one saw a butterfly and he began to race.
(*Bend down second finger.*)
This one saw a cat and he began to chase.
(*Bend down third finger.*)
This one tried to catch his tail and he went round and round.
(*Bend down fourth finger.*)
This one was so quiet, he never made a sound.
(*Bend down thumb.*)

Poem

My Dog Rags

I have a dog and his name is Rags.
He eats so much that his tummy sags.
His ears flip-flop,
(*Place hands on either side of your head.*)
And his tail wig-wags,
(*Wiggly your hips.*)
And when he walks he goes zig-zag.
(*Cross your arms.*)
He goes flip-flop, wig-wag, zig-zag.
(*Repeat with motions three times.*)
I love Rags and he loves me.

Dog Tubey

Parts You'll Need

- Small Tube Cover (Brown)
- Dog Tummy (Tan)
- Dog Collar (Black)
- 2 Dog Ears (Tan)
- Dog Tongue (Red)
- Dog Muzzle (Tan)
- Dog Head (Brown)
- 2 Dog Feet (Tan)
- Dog Tail (Brown)

Materials You'll Need

- half cardboard tube, 2¼ inches tall
- construction paper
- scissors
- glue
- black marker
- single hole punch

Directions

1. Cover the tube with the brown tube cover. Overlap the ends and glue them together.

2. Glue the dog's tummy in the middle of the tube.

3. Glue the collar so it just overlaps the tummy.

4. Hole punch a yellow dot for the tag. Glue it to the collar.

5. Glue an ear to each side of the dog's head.

6. Glue the tongue to the bottom of the head. Glue the muzzle just over the tongue.

7. Hole punch one black dot for the nose. Glue it to the muzzle. Use the marker to add three black dots on each side of the muzzle.

8. Hole punch two white dots for the eyes. Use the marker to draw on the pupils. Glue the eyes on.

9. Glue the head to the dog's body so it just overlaps the collar.

10. Draw paws on the dog's feet. Glue the feet on.

11. Glue the tail to the back of the dog.

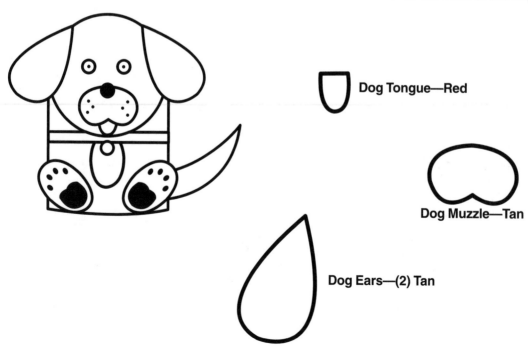

Dog Tongue—Red

Dog Muzzle—Tan

Dog Ears—(2) Tan

Dog Tubey (continued)

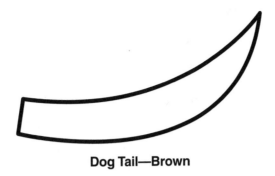

Dog Tail—Brown

Dog Tummy—Tan

Dog Feet—(2) Tan

Dog Collar—Black

Dog Head—Brown

Johnny Appleseed

John Chapman was born on September 26, 1774. He is better known as Johnny Appleseed. He spent 49 years of his life in the American wilderness planting apple seeds and creating orchards in Illinois, Indiana, Kentucky, Pennsylvania and Ohio. Some of the trees still bear apples today. Celebrate the arrival of fall with this fun storytime.

Books to Enjoy

Johnny Appleseed by Rosemary and Stephen Vincent Benét. Margaret K. McElderry Books, 2001. (PK–2) A poem describing Johnny Appleseed's appearance and actions.

Mighty Tree by Dick Gackenbach. Harcourt, 1992. (PK) Three seeds grow into three kinds of beautiful trees, and each one serves a different purpose in nature and for people.

The Seasons of Arnold's Apple Tree by Gail Gibbons. Harcourt Brace Jovanovich, 1984. (K–2) As the seasons pass, Arnold enjoys a variety of activities as a result of his apple tree. Includes a recipe for apple pie and a description of how an apple cider press works.

The Apple Pie Tree by Zoe Hall. Scholastic, 1996. (PK–1) Describes an apple tree as it grows leaves and produces its fruit, while robins make a nest, lay eggs and raise a family in its branches. Minimum text and large, colorful illustrations. Includes a recipe for apple pie.

Johnny Appleseed: My Story by David Lee Harrison. Random House, 2001. (1–3) Johnny Appleseed's life is presented in the form of a tale told to an eager family he visits in his travels.

Be a Friend to Trees by Patricia Lauber. HarperCollins, 1994. (1–3) Discusses the importance of trees as sources of food, oxygen and other essential uses.

Have You Seen Trees? by Joanne Oppenheim. Scholastic, 1995. (K–3) Bright illustrations enhance this story about trees.

Fingerplay

Way up high in the apple tree,
(Point up.)
Two big apples were looking at me.
(Make two circles with hands.)
I shook that tree as hard as I could,
(Both hands shake tree.)
Down came the apples. Mmm! Were they good!
(Rub tummy.)

Act it Out

Dig a hole. Drop in a seed. Cover it with dirt. Water it with the watering can. Shine the sun down on it. See it sprout, then grow to a big tree with apples!

Flannel Board

Flannel pieces you will need:

- tree branch (brown)
- apple blossoms (pink)
- leaves (green)
- apples (red)

Give each child a different flannel piece to help you demonstrate the seasons. Put up the bare branch. Have the children with the blossoms come up and add them. Then add the leaves. The apples take the place of the blossoms. Then take down the apples to eat later. Take the leaves away and the branch is bare again.

Hint: Place the apple pieces in a bag as you remove them. When you are done with the demonstration, reach into the bag and pull out fresh apple slices for everyone!

Johnny Appleseed Tubey

Parts You'll Need

- Johnny Appleseed's Face (Peach)
- Johnny Appleseed's Overalls (Brown)
- Johnny Appleseed's Shirt (White)
- Johnny Appleseed's Saucepan Hat (Gray)
- Johnny Appleseed's Pan Handle (Gray)
- 2 Johnny Appleseed's Sleeves (White)
- 2 Johnny Appleseed's Hands (Peach)
- Apple (Red)
- Apple Stem (Brown)
- Johnny Appleseed's Beard (Dark Brown)

Materials You'll Need

- cardboard tube, 4½ inches tall
- construction paper
- scissors
- scallop-edge scissors
- glue
- black marker
- single hole punch

Directions

1. Glue the face along the top edge of the tube. Overlap the ends and glue them together.

2. Glue on the white shirt so it slightly overlaps the face.

3. Glue on the overalls so they match up with the top of the shirt and the bottom of the tube.

4. Scallop the edge of the beard and glue it on. It should overlap the top of the overalls.

5. Glue the hands to the ends of the sleeves.

6. Glue each sleeve to one side of the tube, next to the overall straps.

7. Glue the stem to the apple.

8. Fold the arms toward the front and glue them to the apple.

9. Fit the saucepan hat around the top of the tube and glue the ends together.

10. Fold the handle along the fold line. Glue the folded edge to the side of the hat.

11. Hole punch two blue dots for the eyes. Use the marker to draw on black pupils and a mouth. Glue on the eyes.

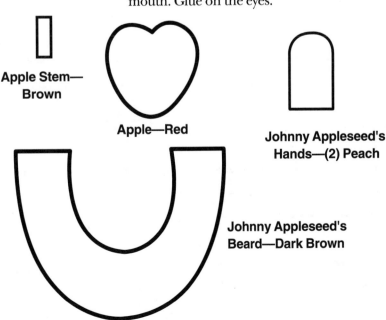

Apple Stem—
Brown

Apple—Red

Johnny Appleseed's
Hands—(2) Peach

Johnny Appleseed's
Beard—Dark Brown

Johnny Appleseed Tubey (continued)

Johnny Appleseed's Face—Peach

Johnny Appleseed's Saucepan Hat—Gray

Johnny Appleseed's Overalls—Brown

Johnny Appleseed's Shirt—White

Fold

Johnny Appleseed's Pan
Handle—Gray

Johnny Appleseed's Sleeves—
(2) White

Cats

Black cats are symbols of Halloween. Make a Black Cat Tubey for Halloween or make a cat the color of your own cat or one you know.

Books to Enjoy

Scary, Scary Halloween by Eve Bunting. Scholastic, 1989. (K–2) A band of trick-or-treaters and a mother cat and her kittens spend a very scary Halloween.

Mrs. McTats and Her Houseful of Cats by Alyssa Satin Capucilli. Margaret K. McElderry Books, 2001. (PK–1) A woman with a single cat named Abner makes room for 24 more cats and a puppy she names Zoom.

Millions of Cats by Wanda Gag. Putnam, 1996. (1–3) Newbery Award Winner. How can a man and his wife choose their favorite cat from a choice of millions and trillions of cats?

Clarence the Copy Cat by Patricia Lakin. Doubleday, 2002. (PK–2) Clarence, a cat who does not want to hurt mice or any other creatures, does not feel welcome anywhere until he discovers the Barnstable Library.

Halloween Cats by Jean Marzollo. Scholastic, 1992. (K–3) Rollicking rhymes about a group of mischievous trick-or-treating cats and delight-fully spunky illustrations, make this a best bet for Halloween.

Halloween Mice by Bethany Roberts. Clarion, 1995. (PK–K) Four Halloween mice dress up in costumes for a midnight romp in the pumpkin patch—but they don't count on a Halloween cat.

The Cat in the Hat by Dr. Seuss. Random House, 1997. (1–2) The most famous cat of all disrupts the house when Sally and her brother are home alone.

This and That by Julie Sykes. Farrar, Straus and Giroux, 1996. (PK–2) Curious about a cat's behavior when she starts borrowing things from them, the farm animals follow her to the stable where they make an interesting discovery.

Ginger by Charlotte Voake. Candlewick Press, 1997. (PK–1) When Ginger the cat gets fed up with her owner's new kitten, it takes a drastic event to make the two of them friends.

Act it Out

What can cats do? *(Walk on four legs, slurp milk, scratch with claws, sleep, hunt for mice, etc.)*

What sound does a cat make? *(Meow, purr, hiss.)*

Rhyme

Three Little Kittens

The three little kittens, they lost their mittens and they began to cry.

"Oh mother dear, see here, see here, our mittens we have lost!"

"What? Lost your mittens? You naughty kittens! Then you shall have no pie!"

Meow, Meow, Meow, Meow, "You shall have no pie!"

The three little kittens, they found their mittens and they began to cry.

"Oh mother dear, see here, see here, our mittens we have found!"

"What? Found your mittens? You good little kittens! Then you shall have some pie!"

Purr, Purr, Purr, Purr, "You shall have some pie!"

Fingerplay

Five Little Kittens

Five little kittens napping on the floor,
(Hold up five fingers.)
One chased a mouse and then there were four.
(Hold up four fingers.)

Four little kittens napping quietly,
One chased a ball and then there were three.
(Hold up three fingers.)

Three little kittens napping just like you,
One chased a leaf and then there were two.
(Hold up two fingers.)

Two little kittens napping in the sun,
One chased a bug and then there was one.
(Hold up one finger.)

One little kitten napping all alone,
One chased YOU! and then there were none.
(One finger points to you.)

Black Cat Tubey

Parts You'll Need

- Small Tube Cover (Black)
- Cat's Head (Black)
- Cat's Tail (Black)
- Cat's Ears (Black)
- Cat's Boots (Black)

Materials You'll Need

- half cardboard tube, 2¼ inches tall
- construction paper
- scissors
- glue
- white colored pencil or crayon
- single hole punch

Directions

1. Cover the tube with the black tube cover. Overlap the ends and glue them together.

2. Outline the boots with the white colored pencil or crayon.

3. With the tube sitting upright, line the boots up to the tube bottom and glue them on.

4. Glue the ears onto the head.

5. Hole punch two yellow dots for the eyes and one pink dot for nose. Glue them to the head.

6. Use the pencil or crayon to draw on the whiskers and a mouth.

7. Glue on the head so it sticks up a little over the top of the tube.

8. Glue the tail to the back of the tube, so it sticks out at one side.

Cat's Boots—Black

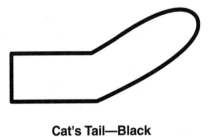

Cat's Tail—Black

Cat's Ears— (2) Black

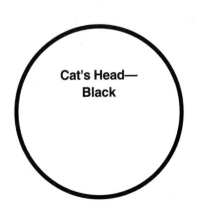

Cat's Head— Black

Spiders

Spiders spinning their webs make a fun storytime for Halloween or anytime.

Books to Enjoy

The Very Busy Spider by Eric Carle. Philomel Books, 1984. (PK–2) The farm animals try to keep a busy spider from spinning, but she keeps working and creates a beautiful and useful web.

Be Nice to Spiders by Margaret Bloy Graham. HarperCollins, 1999. (K–2) Children learn that spiders are very useful when a zookeeper discovers lots of problems after he cleans away all the spiders.

The Spider and the Fly by Mary Botham Howitt. Simon & Schuster, 2002. (1–3) An illustrated version of the nineteenth century English poem about a wily spider and a gullible fly.

Miss Spider series by David Kirk. Scholastic. (PK–2) The adventures of Miss Spider.

The Halloween Showdown by Eileen Ross. Holiday House, Inc., 1999 (K–2) When Grizzorka the Witch snatches Tabitha for her new Halloween cat, Grandmother Katt dons a pumpkin helmet and declares war with the help of Spider, Frog and Bat.

The Best Halloween Hunt Ever by John Speirs. Scholastic, 2000. (PK–K) At school, in the pumpkin patch and all around the town are hidden pumpkins, spiders and bats for the reader to find.

The Itsy Bitsy Spider by Iza Trapani. Scholastic, 1996. (PK) Delightful illustrations accompany the original verse plus a few more. The spider encounters obstacles as she tries to make her way to the top of a tree to spin her web.

Halloween Has Boo! by Harriet Ziefert. Handprint Books, 2002. (PK–1) Romp through Halloween with rhymes of spiders and pumpkins that will bring smiles to all ages.

Song

Bugs

Oh, there ain't no bugs on me,
There ain't no bugs on me,
There may be bugs on some of you mugs,
But there ain't no bugs on me!

Thumbprint Bugs

Press the children's thumbs in ink pads and make thumbprints on paper. Clean their hands, then draw on bug legs and antennae.

Fingerplay

The itsy bitsy spider,
Climbed up the water spout.
(Crawl fingers up.)
Down came the rain,
(Wiggle fingers down.)
And washed the spider out.
(Flick both hands away.)
Out came the sun,
And dried up all the rain.
(Both hands make a sun overhead.)
And the itsy bitsy spider,
Crawled up the spout again.
(Crawl fingers up.)

Note: To simplify the spider crawl, try holding your left arm up and using the fingers of your right hand to climb up your left arm.

Nursery Rhyme

Little Miss Muffet

Little Miss Muffet sat on a tuffet,
Eating her curds and whey.
Along came a spider and sat down beside her,
And frightened Miss Muffet away!

Spider Tubey

Parts You'll Need

- Small Tube Cover (Black)
- 2 Spider Legs (Black)
- Spider Head (Black)

Materials You'll Need

- half cardboard tube, 2¼ inches tall
- construction paper
- scissors
- glue
- single hole punch
- black marker

Directions

1. Cover the tube with the black tube cover. Overlap the ends and glue them together.

2. Fold the spider legs along the fold lines. Glue one folded edge to each side of the spider.

3. Hole punch two light green dots for the eyes and glue them onto the head.

4. Glue the head onto the front of the tube.

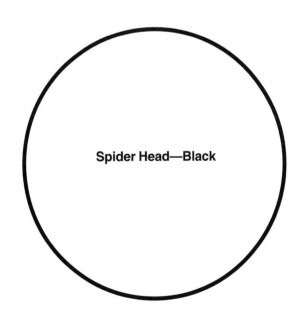

Spider Head—Black

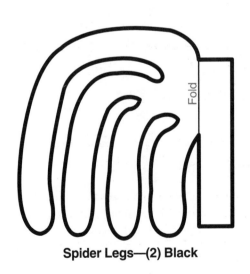

Spider Legs—(2) Black

Pocahontas

Pocahontas was an Indian princess who was born around 1596. She was the daughter of Chief Powhatan of the Algonquian Indians. Pocahontas is most famous for reportedly saving the life of English Captain John Smith. She also promoted peace between the Powhatans and the English colonists. Use this storytime to help your children learn about Pocahontas as well as some Native American customs.

Books to Enjoy

Young Pocahontas, Indian Princess by Anne Benjamin. Troll, 1992. (PK–K) Part of the Troll First-Start Biography series. A simple biography of the seventeenth-century Indian princess who befriended Captain John Smith and the English settlers at Jamestown.

Pocahontas by Jan Gleiter and Kathleen Thompson. Steck-Vaughn, 1995. (K–3) Part of the First Biographies series. The life story of Pocahontas retold for young readers.

The Story of Pocahontas by Caryn Jenner. DK Publishing, Inc., 2000. (1–3) Examines the life of the Indian princess and her contact with English settlers, especially John Smith.

The True Story of Pocahontas by Lucille Recht Penner. Random House, 1994. (1–3) Part of the Step Into Reading series. Simple biography of the Indian princess.

Pocahontas by Lucia Raatma. Compass Point Books, 2002. (2–3) A simple biography of Pocahontas.

Set the Scene

Set out books about early settlers and Native Americans. Display Native American artifacts such as arrowheads, baskets, etc.

Counting Song

Ten Little Indians

(Use fingers to count up and down.)

One little, two little, three little Indians,
Four little, five little, six little Indians,
Seven little, eight little, nine little Indians,
Ten little Indian boys.

Ten little, nine little, eight little Indians,
Seven little, six little, five little Indians,
Four little, three little, two little Indians,
One little Indian boy.

Note: Can substitute "Indian girls."

Pocahontas Tubey

Parts You'll Need

- Pocahontas's Face (Medium Brown)
- Pocahontas's Headband (Brown)
- Pocahontas's Dress (Tan)
- Pocahontas's Braid Bands (Brown)
- Pocahontas's Feathers (White)
- Pocahontas's Hair (Black)

Materials You'll Need

- cardboard tube, 4½ inches tall
- construction paper
- scissors
- glue
- black marker
- single hole punch

Directions

1. Glue the face along the top edge of the tube. Overlap the ends and glue them together.

2. Cut slits along the bottom of the dress as indicated on the pattern. Glue the dress along the bottom edge of the tube.

3. Glue on the hair so the braids are in the front. Overlap the ends in the back.

4. Glue the bands onto the bottom of the braids.

5. Glue the headband along the top edge of the tube.

6. Glue the feathers to the back of the head.

7. Hole punch eight black dots to make the necklace. Glue them in place.

8. Hole punch two brown dots for the eyes. Use the marker to draw on black pupils and a mouth. Glue on the eyes.

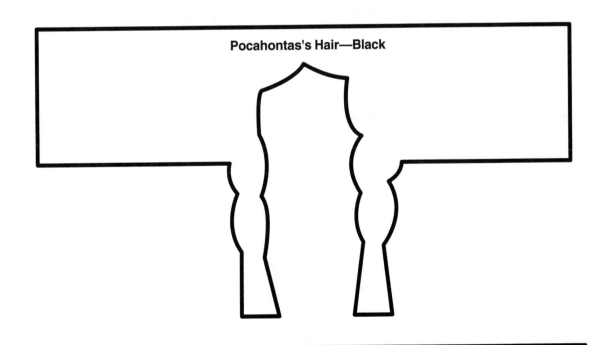

Pocahontas's Hair—Black

Pocahontas's Headband—Brown

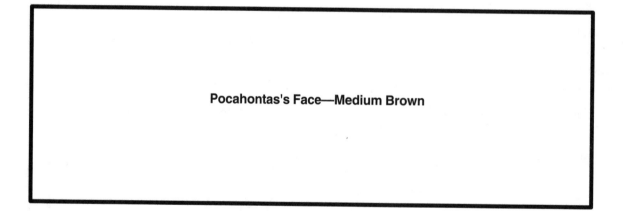

Pocahontas's Dress—Tan

Cut Lines

Pocahontas's Face—Medium Brown

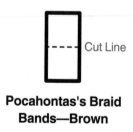

Cut Line

**Pocahontas's Braid
Bands—Brown**

Cut Lines

Pocahontas's Feathers—White

Thanksgiving

The first Thanksgiving was celebrated in 1621 when the colonists gave thanks for a bountiful harvest. They invited the local Indians. The colonists continued the tradition until America gained independence, then Congress recommended that one annual day of thanksgiving should be set aside for the whole nation. It is now celebrated on the fourth Thursday in November. Celebrate the harvest with this Thanksgiving storytime.

Books to Enjoy

Thank You, Sarah: The Woman Who Saved Thanksgiving by Laurie Halse Anderson. Simon & Schuster, 2002. (1–3) Relates how Sarah Hale persuaded President Lincoln to transform Thanksgiving Day into a national holiday.

A Turkey for Thanksgiving by Eve Bunting. Clarion Books, 1991. (PK–2) Turkey gets the wrong idea when Mr. Moose tells him that he and Mrs. Moose want him for Thanksgiving dinner.

Over the River and Through the Wood by Lydia Marie Child. Henry Holt, 1996. (PK–1) An illustrated version of the poem and song about a journey through the snow to grandmother's house for Thanksgiving dinner.

Gracias, the Thanksgiving Turkey by Joy Cowley. Scholastic, 1996. (PK–3) Trouble begins when Miguel starts to get attached to a turkey that his papa is fattening up for Thanksgiving dinner.

Today is Thanksgiving by P. K. Hallinan. Ideals Children's Books, 2002. (PK–1) A charming story in rhyme that gives a good explanation of Thanksgiving for very young children.

'Twas the Night Before Thanksgiving by Dav Pilkey. Orchard Books, 1990. (PK–3) Schoolchildren on a field trip to the farm save the lives of eight turkeys in this humorous story inspired by "The Night Before Christmas."

Set the Scene

Ask the children to name the things that they are thankful for. Talk about the first Thanksgiving feast. What do you think they ate? What do you eat now on Thanksgiving?

Fingerplay

Five Fat Turkeys

Start with your hands behind your back.

Five fat turkeys are we,
(Show five fingers on one hand.)
We slept all night in a tree,
(Put hand up high.)
When the cook came around,
(One hand stays up high, the other shows one finger.)
We couldn't be found,
(Make one finger look all around and shake head.)
And that's why we're here, you see.
(Cook goes away, turkeys come back down.)

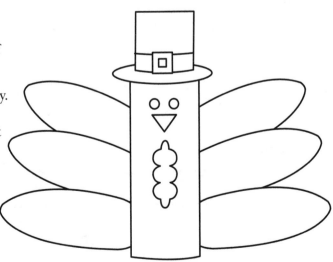

Turkey Tubey

Parts You'll Need

- Basic Tube Cover (Brown)
- Basic Hat Pieces 1 and 2 (Black)
- Turkey Wattle (Red)
- Turkey Beak (Orange)
- Turkey Hatband (Gray)
- Turkey Hatband Buckle (Yellow)
- Turkey Feathers (1 each of Red, Yellow, Green, Orange, Purple and Brown)

Materials You'll Need

- cardboard tube, 4½ inches tall
- construction paper
- scissors
- glue
- black marker
- single hole punch

Directions

1. Cover the tube with the brown tube cover. Overlap the ends and glue them together.

2. Hole punch two black eyes and glue them about ¾ inch down from the top of the tube.

3. Glue the beak on under the eyes.

4. Glue the wattle on under the beak.

5. Glue the feathers to the back in a fan effect. There should be three on each side.

6. Make the hat following the instructions on page 6.

7. Glue the hatband around the hat.

8. Glue the buckle at the front of the hatband. Set the hat on the turkey's head.

Variation: Substitute fall leaves for your Turkey's feathers.

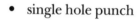

Turkey Beak—Orange

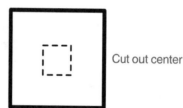

Cut out center

Turkey Hatband Buckle—Yellow

Turkey Wattle—Red

Turkey Feathers—(1 each) Red, Yellow, Green, Orange, Purple, Brown

Turkey Hatband—Gray

Gingerbread Men

Start your winter holiday celebration with this tasty storytime.

Books to Enjoy

Gingerbread Baby by Jan Brett. Putnam, 1999. (PK–1) The traditional tale of the escaping gingerbread cookie, but with a surprise ending.

The Gingerbread Boy by Paul Galdone. Seabury Press, 1975. (PK–3) A freshly baked gingerbread boy leads everyone on a merry chase until the sly fox outsmarts them all and eats the cookie.

A Cow, a Bee, a Cookie, and Me by Meredith Hooper. Kingfisher, 1997. (PK–1) Ben's grandmother explains where the ingredients originated as she bakes honey cookies. Includes recipe.

The Gingerbread Man by Carol Jones. Houghton Mifflin, 2002. (PK–2) A freshly baked gingerbread man escapes when he is taken out of the oven. Includes recipe.

Who Took the Cookies from the Cookie Jar? by Bonnie Lass and Philemon Sturges. Little, Brown, 2000. (PK–2) A skunk tries to find out which of his animal friends stole the cookies.

The Best Smelling Christmas Book Ever by Laura Rader. Little Simon, 1997. (PK–K) A sniff and smell book about the baking and building of a gingerbread house.

Set the Scene

Use a cookie cutter to outline the gingerbread shape onto construction paper. Cut the gingerbread men out and make bookmarks or nametags for everyone.

Poem

Gingerbread Man

I'm a gingerbread cookie.
I taste mighty good.

You could catch me and eat me,
If you think you could!
Run, run, as fast as you can!
You can't catch me, I'm the gingerbread man!

Song

Eat Your Gingerbread Boy

(Sung to the tune: "Row, Row, Row, Your Boat")

Eat, eat, your Gingerbread Boy,
Before he runs away.
Faster, faster, faster please,
Don't let him get away.

Catch, catch the Gingerbread Boy,
Catch him, yes, today.
Faster, faster, faster still,
For he has run away.

Say bye-bye to the Gingerbread Boy,
Say good-bye today.
Say so long for he is gone,
The fox ate him today.

After the Program

Serve each child a small gingerbread cookie.

Gingerbread Man Tubey

Parts You'll Need

- Small Tube Cover (Brown)
- 2 Gingerbread Man Arms (Brown)
- Frosting Design (2 of each in White)

Materials You'll Need

- half cardboard tube, 2¼ inches tall
- construction paper
- scissors
- glue
- single hole punch

Directions

1. Cover the tube with the brown tube cover. Overlap the ends and glue them together.

2. Fold the arms along the fold line. Glue a folded edge to each side of the body.

3. Glue one large frosting design piece along the top of the tube and one along the bottom. Glue one small frosting piece to each arm.

4. Hole punch two white dots for the buttons. Glue them to the front of the gingerbread man.

5. Hole punch two black dots for the eyes, then glue them on. Use the marker to draw on a mouth.

Gingerbread Man Arms—(2) Brown

Frosting Design, Small—(2) White

Frosting Design, Large—(2) White

Elves

Elves and fairies fascinate children, especially at Christmastime. Use this storytime as another way to celebrate the holidays.

Books to Enjoy

Diane Goode's Book of Giants and Little People by Diane Goode. Dutton Children's Books, 1997. (PK–4) Tales, nursery rhymes and poems featuring characters that are extraordinarily large or small, such as giants, elves and fairies.

The Elves and the Shoemaker by the Brothers Grimm, retold by Paul Galdone. Clarion Books, 1984. (K–3) A poor shoemaker becomes successful with the help of two elves who finish his shoes during the night.

How Santa Lost His Job by Stephen Krensky. Simon & Schuster, 2001. (K–3) Muckle the elf tries to replace Santa's delivery system with his invention, the Deliverator.

My "E" Sound Box by Jane Belk Moncure. Child's World, 2001 . (PK–1) Little elves are featured as a little boy places items that begin with the letter "E" in a box.

The Forgotten Helper: A Christmas Story by Lorrie Moore. Delacorte Press, 2000. (PK–1) When Santa's grouchiest elf is left at the house of a bad little girl, he must find a way to improve her behavior so that Santa will return for him.

The Golden Book Treasury of Elves and Fairies selected by Jane Werner. Golden Books, 1999. (PK–4) Beautifully illustrated collection of poems and stories of the little people.

Set the Scene

Talk about losing things. Have you ever lost a toy and couldn't find it again? Show an empty spool of thread, a bottle cap or other small item. Ask if these are things you would throw away. Then tell how the bottle cap could be a stool and a spool could be a table for an elf family. What other things could they use?

Poem

Elves in the Shady Glen

Somewhere down in the shady glen,
Lives a group of tiny men.
They borrow things from you and me,
And take them where you cannot see.

If you have lost a toy or ball,
An elf man may have come to call.
He comes in quiet as a mouse,
And takes your toys back to his house.
And when he gets them home, you see,
He makes things for his family.

So don't be sad if you can't find,
Your toy car or a piece of twine.
The elves can use them all again,
Somewhere down in the shady glen.

Standing Fingerplay

Santa's Elf

I wish I was Santa's elf,
(Squat low.)
And lived at the North Pole.
(Stand tall and point up high.)
I'd see Santa every day,
(Both hands make eyeglasses.)
And lots of ice and snow! Brrr!
(Cross both arms and shiver.)

After the Program

Serve small treats (raisins, mini marshmallows, etc.) on very small plates for an elf snack. For the plate, cut a small drinking cup down to the base.

Elf Tubey

Parts You'll Need

- Small Tube Cover (Peach)
- Elf's Under Clothing (Light Green)
- Elf's Outer Clothing (Green)
- Elf's Vest (Red)
- Elf's Hat (Green)
- Elf's Hat Fur (Red)
- Elf's Hat Tassel (Red)

Materials You'll Need

- half cardboard tube, 2¼ inches tall
- construction paper
- scissors
- glue
- black marker
- single hole punch
- scallop-edge scissors *(optional)*

Directions

1. Cover the tube with the peach tube cover. Overlap the ends and glue them together.

2. Glue the under clothing along the bottom edge of the tube.

3. Glue the outer clothing above the under clothing. Overlap the two pieces so no peach color is showing.

4. Glue the red vest along the top of the outer clothing.

5. Hole punch a green dot for the vest button and glue it on.

6. Scallop the edges of the hat fur and tassel.

7. Glue the fur to the bottom of the hat. Glue the tassel to the top of the hat.

8. Glue the hat to the front of the tube.

9. Hole punch two blue dots for the eyes. Use the marker to draw on black pupils and a mouth. Glue on the eyes.

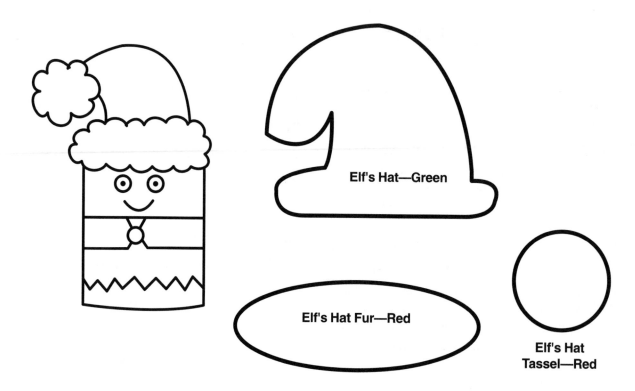

Elf's Hat—Green

Elf's Hat Fur—Red

Elf's Hat Tassel—Red

Elf Tubey (continued)

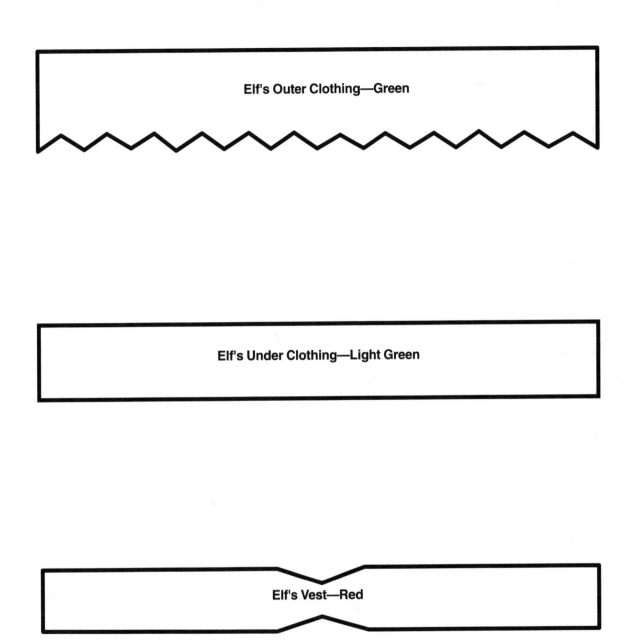

Elf's Outer Clothing—Green

Elf's Under Clothing—Light Green

Elf's Vest—Red

Santa Claus

Travel to the North Pole for a visit with Santa Claus in this merry storytime.

Books to Enjoy

A Taxi Dog Christmas by Debra and Sal Barracca. Dial Books for Young Readers, 1994. (PK–1) Maxi and Jim the taxi driver gladly interrupt their Christmas celebration to lend Santa a hand.

How Santa Claus Had a Long and Difficult Journey Delivering His Presents by Fernando Krahn. Delacorte Press, 1970. (PK–K) Pictures without words show how Santa Claus tries to get airborne after the reindeer break away from their traces.

If You Take a Mouse to the Movies by Laura Joffe Numeroff. HarperCollins, 2000. (PK–2) One thing leads to another if you take a mouse to the movies at Christmastime.

Auntie Claus and the Key to Christmas by Elise Primavera. Harcourt, 2002. (K–2) When Chris expresses doubt about the existence of Santa Claus, his older sister Sophie reveals that their aunt is Santa's sister and helper. Then she sends him on a strange journey. Sequel to *Auntie Claus.*

The Night Before Christmas by Robert Sabuda and Clement Clarke Moore. Simon & Schuster, 2002. (K–3) Clement Clarke Moore's classic tale of *The Night Before Christmas* is brought to pop-up life in this new edition.

Shhh! by Julie Sykes. Scholastic, 1998. (PK–3) Although it is his favorite night of the year, Santa Claus tries very hard not to wake up the children of the world as he makes his deliveries on Christmas Eve.

The Polar Express by Chris Van Allsburg. Houghton Mifflin, 1985. (K–2) A magical train ride on Christmas Eve takes a boy to the North Pole to receive a special gift from Santa Claus.

Jingle Bells

Tie curling ribbon through two small jingle bells, then tie the ribbons to a small candy cane. Make one for each child. Sing "Jingle Bells" and have the children shake their candy canes as you sing. Then let the children take their bells home.

Song

Santa Claus is Coming to Town

Oh! You better watch out,
You better not cry,
You better not pout,
I'm telling you why.
Santa Claus is coming to town!

He's making a list,
He's checking it twice,
Gonna find out who's naughty or nice.
Santa Claus is coming to town!

He sees you when you're sleeping,
He knows when you're awake.
He knows if you've been bad or good,
So be good for goodness sake!

Fingerplay

Santa Claus

Here is the chimney,
(Make a fist, enclose thumb.)
Here is the top.
(Place palm on top of fist.)
Open the lid,
(Remove top hand.)
And out Santa will pop.
(Pop up thumb.)

Santa Claus is Back!

Two merry blue eyes,
(Point to eyes.)
A cute little nose,
(Point to nose.)
A long, snowy beard.
(Stroke beard.)
Two cheeks like a rose.
(Touch cheeks with both hands.)
A round, chubby form,
(Rub stomach.)
A big, bulging sack,
(Bend over, hold "sack.")
Hurrah for old Santa!
(Clap hands.)
We're glad that he's back!

Santa's Shop

Five busy elves at work in Santa's shop,
(Hold up five fingers.)
Hammer, hammer, hammer without a stop.
(Make fists with both hands and pound right hand on top of left hand.)
One little elf grew so very tired,
(Hold up one finger, yawn and stretch.)
Hammer, hammer, hammer—he closed his eyes.
(Make hammering motion very slowly and close your eyes.)
Wake up! It's Christmas!
(Open eyes.)

Repeat fingerplay with one less elf each time.

Santa Claus Tubey

Parts You'll Need

- Basic Tube Cover (Red)
- Santa's Face (Peach)
- Santa's Belt (Black)
- Santa's Belt Buckle (Yellow)
- Santa's Beard (White)
- Santa's Mustache (White)
- Santa's Hat (Red)
- Santa's Hat Tassel (White)
- Santa's Hat Fur (White)

Materials You'll Need

- cardboard tube, 4½ inches tall
- construction paper
- scissors
- glue
- scallop-edge scissors
- black marker
- single hole punch

Directions

1. Cover the tube with the red tube cover. Overlap the ends and glue them together.

2. Glue Santa's face along the top edge of the tube.

3. Scallop the edges of the beard, mustache, fur and tassel.

4. Glue the beard along the top edge of the tube. Glue the mustache along the inside curve of the beard.

5. Glue on the belt, then the buckle.

6. Glue the fur to the bottom of the hat and the tassel to the tip of the hat.

7. Glue the hat to the top of Santa's head.

8. Hole punch two blue dots for the eyes. Use a marker to draw on black pupils. Glue on the eyes.

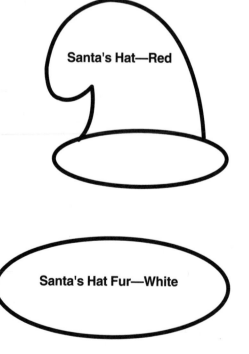

Santa's Hat—Red

Santa's Mustache—
White

Santa's Hat
Tassel—White

Santa's Hat Fur—White

Santa Claus Tubey (continued)

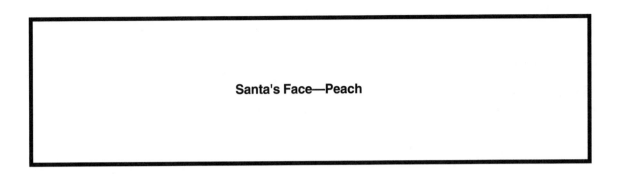

Santa's Face—Peach

Santa's Belt—Black

Cut out center

Santa's Belt Buckle—Yellow

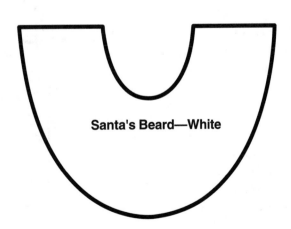

Santa's Beard—White

Angels

Angels are often placed at the top of a Christmas tree. Use this storytime to celebrate another Christmas tradition.

Books to Enjoy

An Angel Just Like Me by Mary Hoffman. Dial Books for Young Readers, 1997. (PK–2) An African American child wonders why all the Christmas tree angels look alike and sets out to find an angel that looks just like him.

The Snow Angel by Angela McAllister. Lothrop, Lee & Shepard Books, 1993. (K–2) Elsa thinks her brother Jack imagines seeing a snow angel until she meets the angel herself.

Albert and the Angels by Leslie Norris. Farrar, Straus and Giroux, 2000. (PK–K) As Christmas approaches, a young boy and his talking dog, that only he can hear, try their best to find a replacement for the special medallion that his mother lost long ago.

Hark! The Aardvark Angels Sing by Teri Sloat. Putnam, 2001. (PK–3) A fantastical version of the traditional Christmas carol that features aardvark angels who assist mail carriers in delivering the mounds of Christmas mail.

What Night do the Angels Wander? by Phoebe Stone. Little, Brown, 1998. (PK–1) Rhyming text describes the one night of the year when the angels come together to celebrate with the children and animals of the earth.

Snow Angels

Make an angel in the snow. Lie down on your back and stretch your arms out to each side. Move your outstretched arms up and down to leave an angel print. If it doesn't snow where you live, try making an angel in the sand.

Set the Scene

Use a cookie cutter to outline an angel shape onto construction paper. Cut the angels out and make bookmarks or nametags for everyone.

Song

Five Little Candles

Five little candles twinkling on the tree.
The first one said, "What do you see?"
The second one said, "I see Santa big and jolly."
The third one said, "I see Christmas wreaths and holly."
The fourth one said, "What do you hear?"
The fifth one said, "Angel bells ringing loud and clear."
A very Merry Christmas and a Happy New Year.

Angel Tubey

Parts You'll Need

- Basic Tube Cover (Dark Pink)
- Angel's Face (Light Pink)
- Angel's Hair (Light Brown)
- Angel's Wings (Yellow)
- Angel's Headband (Dark Pink)

Materials You'll Need

- cardboard tube, 4½ inches tall
- construction paper
- scissors
- glue
- black marker
- pencil
- star hole punch or gold stars
- single hole punch
- scallop-edge scissors *(optional)*
- glitter, stars, etc. *(optional)*

Directions

1. Cover the tube with the dark pink tube cover. Overlap the ends and glue them together.

2. Scallop the bottom edge of the face if desired.

3. Glue the face along the top edge of the tube.

4. Scallop the edges of the wings and decorate the wings with glitter, stars, etc., if desired.

5. Glue the wings to the back of the tube.

6. Glue one star hole punch to the front of the Angel's robe.

7. Cut slits in the hair as indicated on the pattern. Glue the hair along the top edge of the tube. Curl the hair up by wrapping each strip around a pencil.

8. Glue the headband along the top edge of the tube.

9. Hole punch eight stars for the headband and glue them on.

10. Hole punch two light blue dots for the eyes. Use the marker to draw on black pupils and a mouth. Glue the eyes on.

Variation: Change the color of the face, hair and eyes to make an angel "just like you." Or make an angel wreath with Angel Tubeys of various colors.

Angel's Headband—Dark Pink

Angel Tubey (continued)

Angel's Face—Light Pink

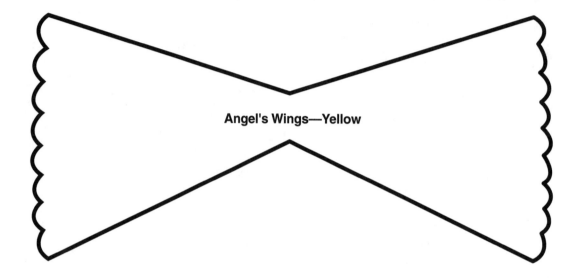

Angel's Wings—Yellow

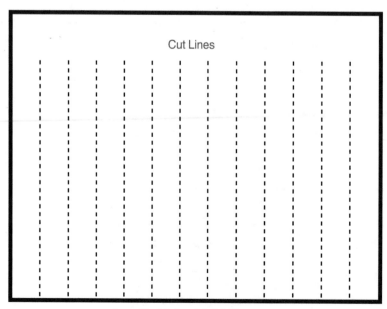

Cut Lines

Angel's Hair—Light Brown